SIGNATURE DISHES

WINE AND FOOD OF CALIFORNIA'S CENTRAL COAST WINERIES

by Tricia Volk

&

Mary Tartaglione

with forward by
Madeleine Kamman

•

Design & Illustration
Joanne Stevens

Published by
SANDCASTLE PUBLISHING

Publisher's Cataloging in Publication
(Prepared by Quality Books Inc.)
Volk, Tricia and Tartaglione, Mary.
      Signature Dishes : wine and food of California's Central Coast wineries / by Tricia Volk and Mary Tartaglione ; with foreword by Madeleine Kamman ; design & illustration, Joanne Stevens.
      p. cm.
      Includes index.
      Preassigned LCCN: 94-65671.
      ISBN 1-883995-04-3
      1. Cookery, American--California style. 2. Wine and winemaking--California.   I. Tartaglione, Mary. II. Title.

TX715.2.C34V65 1994   641.59794
                                              QBI94-676

Printed and bound in the United States of America

96 95 94   10 9 8 7 6 5 4 3 2 1

To, Mom,

whose kitchen

was always open

for culinary

exploration.

✕

5 August 1994

Here's a toast to the Central

Coast. Enjoy!

Tricia Valk
and

[signature]

ACKNOWLEDGEMENTS

We would like to acknowledge the following people for their valuable assistance with *Signature Dishes*. Your efforts are greatly appreciated.

Susan Baldwin *for the photos*

Samir Barudi *for the computer expertise*

Jo Ann Bell *for the encouragement*

Heather Eller *for the word processing*

Cate Heneghan *for the proof reading*

Toni Impala *for the great recipe*

Madeleine Kamman *for being receptive to our request*

Don Reynolds *for the ongoing friendship*

Renee Rolle-Whatley *for recognizing a good thing*

Joanne Stevens *for the artistic expertise*

John Tartaglione *for the critical eye*

Ken Volk *for the input and support*

The Wineries without whose contribution
this would not have been possible

Contents

*U*pon arriving from my native France in early 1960, my husband Alan and I established our home in diverse regions of the North East. It was in the Boston area that I was to do most of my culinary work, until 1980 when I returned to France for several years just to "feel the culinary climate." Back in this country by 1984, I reestablished my culinary school and restaurant in the Mount Washington Valley, traveling and guest chefing across the United States at the same time. One of those business trips brought me to the Napa Valley. It was love at first sight, a love that must have been of some intensity, since I now live there, teaching culinary arts to the younger generation of chefs at Beringer Vineyards.

Investigating the diverse scenarios of California became my priority. One of these fascinating trips took me from Monterey to Livermore to see the old vineyards of the late eighteen hundreds. Then, as I came south towards the ocean, I found Paso Robles and Santa Barbara.

Fascinated as I am by geology, I found the area a true paradise of diversity and beauty. Where else can one, in a matter of a half hour, drive through two centuries of history as one passes Mission San Miguel Archangel then almost immediately afterwards, through the center of a petroleum extraction field complete with dinosaur-like pumps and refinery. Where else will a missed turn bring you to the center of a Danish village known as Solvang and a breakfast of Habelskivers, those nice little round pancakes accompanied with a light raspberry jam.

The best surprises yet came from the vineyards established not only in the well-known Livermore Valley, but quite unexpectedly in smaller valleys such as the upper Carmel, the Santa Ynez and the Edna Valleys. The variety of wines grown here is a dream, as the favorite Cabernet Sauvignon and Chardonnay, a number of Rhone Valley varieties, the Chenin of French Loire and the Riesling and the Gewurztraminer of the Alsace grow in plots adjacent to one another. The winemakers have a talent all of their own and the way most of them preserve the characteristics of the fruit from cluster to bottle is impressive whether they elaborate the best red varietals or their excellent white wines, still or bubbly.

Of course, I strongly recommend a visit to all these vineyards, the older ones as well as the younger ones. While the winemakers of both genders produce wines that range from extraordinary to splendid, the cooks do no worse. The fare is wonderful, reflecting the close proximity of the ocean and the generosity of the gardens and fields that have soaked up sun with avidity.

This lovely cookbook is filled with tasty offerings guaranteed to bring the bounty of the Central Coast to your table wherever you are in the United States. Cook up a storm from it, and serve the results of your efforts to a circle of good friends. The foods and wines will so fill your evening with the warmth, beauty and generosity of the California Central Coast, that you are sure to set your mind simply to come, visit, see, and taste for yourself...

PREFACE

Tricia Volk *with* Mary Tartaglione

*I*n the many years I have spent working in the field of culinary arts and teaching cooking classes, and as co-owner of Wild Horse Winery, people often prompted me to write a cookbook. This was especially true for my sister, who wanted to combine her talents as a writer with my knowledge of food.

Off and on for more than ten years we discussed the possibility, but in reality she was busy pursuing a career and I was focused on the winery and my family. There was always something else to do. Then one day in October of 1992, Mary and I were in my kitchen cooking and talking, and the conversation came back to the subject of the Central Coast. I have never been able to fathom why someone wasn't knocking down the door to showcase the wine-and-food lifestyle here. The Central Coast is blessed with many things: natural beauty, a wonderful, unpretentious attitude where warm hospitality prevails, farm-fresh produce, and grape-harvest bounties where excellent vintages are the norm.

So, in a single moment, we decided to take on the project ourselves.

Wine people are unique. There are the one-man-bands, and there are the corporate giants. There are the dilettantes and the mom-and-pop-operations. They share a common bond in that they like to have fun, and are both laid-back and hardworking to the extreme. In any event, they appreciate good food.

This book reflects the winemakers and the wineries of the Central Coast, which stretches from Ventura County, in the South, to Livermore Valley, in the North. We surveyed the wineries in this geographical configuration, and they shared with us their best recipes, all of which passed muster in our test kitchen. They also provided a brief description of the winery and offered a wine-accompaniment suggestion. Hence the title: *Signature Dishes - Wine and Food of California's Central Coast Wineries.*

Seasonal food and wine are the spirit of the book. From the wide array of fish and shellfish from the Pacific Ocean, to the meat, game, and cheeses from the inland ranches, the recipes have it all. This is not to mention the plethora of seasonal fruits and vegetables available at the farmer's markets hosted in many Central Coast towns on a weekly basis.

There is an overwhelming number of main-dish recipes, which we expected as wine is a food beverage. We, however, let the recipes flow in exactly as they may, without controlling the process. We discovered that wine people have a casual approach to cooking - many don't use exact methods and most rarely make a dish the same way twice. Whatever the case, the finished products are meant to be enjoyed with friends. As our personal offering, we have included a "Chef's Contribution" in each of the four sections.

We send out a heart-felt thank you to all of the wineries. They have been incredibly generous with their time and their cooperative attitude. We hope you enjoy using the book as much as we did creating it.

$\int$TARTERS

ALBAN VINEYARDS

Alban Vineyards is California's first winery and vineyard established exclusively for the production of Rhone varieties. Launched in 1985 by John Alban, it was six years before the first wines were produced.

Pioneering new varieties in this country meant starting with only 12 cuttings and meticulously propagating 60,000 vines. Alban Vineyards now has 60 acres in the Edna Valley divided between Viognier, Roussanne and Syrah. Viognier is the world's rarest and most exotic white grape — fewer than 200 total acres exist. Alban's Roussanne is also unusual. Only two wineries currently produce a varietal wine from this wonderful white variety.

Viognier and Roussanne pair so well with food, you will find them unique matches to a wide array of dishes. This salad makes a complete healthy meal. Serve with fresh bread of choice.

CALIFORNIA SALAD NIÇOISE

4 portions

2 pounds fresh asparagus, tough stems removed
1 pound new potatoes, the smallest you can find
4 fresh Ahi tuna steaks, about 2 pounds
Salt and freshly ground black pepper, to taste
6 cups baby organic mixed greens, about 1/4 pound
1 red bell pepper, seeded, and cut into thin strips
1 yellow bell pepper, seeded, and cut into thin strips
2/3 cup Niçoise olives

Dressing
2 tablespoons balsamic vinegar
1 tablespoon fresh lemon juice
Grated zest of 1/2 lemon
1 tablespoon Dijon mustard
1 tablespoon very finely minced shallots or scallions
1 tablespoon Herbs de Provence
1/2 cup extra virgin olive oil
Salt and freshly ground black pepper, to taste

1 Cook the asparagus: In a large kettle bring 2 quarts of water to a boil with some salt. Drop in the asparagus, cover and return to a boil. Uncover at once and simmer for 1 or 2 minutes. The asparagus is done when just tender with the slightest crunch. Drain immediately. Return the asparagus to the kettle and run cold water into it to cool them rapidly, adding a tray of ice cubes. When they are chilled, drain again, pat dry and refrigerate.

2   Cook the potatoes: Place the potatoes in a steamer basket in a saucepan containing 2 inches of water and bring to a boil. Lower the heat to moderate, cover tightly and steam for about 20 minutes, or until cooked through. Taste one to check. Set aside to cool in the refrigerator.

3   Prepare the dressing: In a pint jar, mix the balsamic vinegar, lemon juice, lemon zest, mustard, shallots, Herbs de Provence, olive oil, 1/4 teaspoon salt, and several grindings of pepper. Shake well. Taste for seasoning, adding more lemon juice, salt and pepper, if needed. Set aside at room temperature until needed. Refrigerate excess after using.

4   Cook the Ahi steaks: Preheat the broiler, or light a fire in the barbecue. When the coals are very hot, season the steaks with salt and pepper and brush with a little bit of the salad dressing. Cook until just seared on the outside and turn the steaks to sear the other side. Remove for rare Ahi, or continue to cook for medium or well done. Cover the steaks with aluminum foil to keep warm while assembling the salads.

5   On 4 dinner plates assemble the salads: Make a bed of the greens in the center of each plate. Divide the asparagus, new potatoes, red and yellow bell peppers, and Niçoise olives strategically on each plate, leaving room for the Ahi in the center. Place the fish on each salad. Spoon some dressing over each of the ingredients to moisten, but not soak the salads. Serve as soon as possible.

Wine Suggestion - Serve with Alban Vineyards Viognier or Roussanne.

BYRON VINEYARD AND WINERY

Byron "Ken" Brown is the founder, winemaker and general manager of Byron Vineyard & Winery, one of Santa Barbara County's most prominent wineries.

In 1983 Ken and his wife Deborah Kenly Brown began working with friend and vineyard consultant Dale Hampton to design what is now Byron Vineyard & Winery. They chose the Tepusquet Canyon area of Santa Maria for its rustic beauty and proximity to the 6,000 acres of vineyard found in the cool Santa Maria Valley. Construction began in 1984 — the year of Byron's first harvest. The winery enjoyed early success and gained national recognition for quality Pinot Noir, Chardonnay and Sauvignon Blanc.

In 1990 the Robert Mondavi Winery of Napa Valley acquired Byron Vineyard and Winery and its 125 acres of vineyard. The winery is operated independently of Robert Mondavi Winery under the direction of Ken Brown.

✴ *This stunning salad is from Hoppe's at 901 Restaurant in Morro Bay. It truly is a summer pleasure.*

✿

SUMMER SALMON SALAD
6 portions

Salmon
1 1/2 pounds fresh, local salmon fillet, skinned,
*   pin-boned, and cut into 6 slices*
2 tablespoons extra virgin olive oil
Salt and freshly ground black pepper, to taste

Salad
16 ounces mixed seasonal greens, washed and dried
6 ears sweet corn, blanched, then cut from the cob
1 bunch fresh tarragon, stems removed
1 bunch fresh chervil, stems removed
2 bunches fresh chives, chopped
3 avocados, peeled, seeded, and cut into cubes

Dressing
6 slices bacon, finely minced
3 shallots, peeled, and finely minced
1 2/3 cups Byron Pinot Noir
2 cups shellfish stock or Atlantic brand clam juice
1 cup roasted garlic oil (recipe follows)
1 tablespoon balsamic vinegar, or to taste
Freshly ground black pepper, to taste

Roasted Garlic Oil
1 head garlic, separated into cloves, skin discarded
and cloves flattened with a knife
1 cup extra virgin olive oil

To prepare the salmon

1 Marinate the salmon slices in the olive oil, salt and pepper for 30 minutes.

2 Prepare hot coals for grilling.

To prepare the salad

1 Combine all the salad ingredients together in a large salad bowl. Cover with a slightly damp tea towel and chill.

To prepare the dressing

1 In a large skillet sauté the bacon over medium-high heat until it is crisp and brown. Drain off the fat and add the shallots to the skillet. Cook the shallots until they are slightly brown. Add the Pinot Noir and reduce by one-half. Add the shellfish stock and reduce by one half again. Strain the dressing through a sieve and cool.

To prepare roasted garlic oil

1 Heat a small saucepan over medium-low heat. Add the olive oil and garlic and cook until the garlic is golden brown, about 5 minutes. Be careful not to burn the garlic. Strain the oil through a sieve into the dressing mixture. Season the dressing with the balsamic vinegar and pepper. Chill the dressing slightly.

To finish the salad

1 Grill the salmon slices over the hot coals until the desired doneness is reached. Keep them warm.

2 Pour 2/3 of the salad dressing over the chilled salad ingredients. Toss the salad gently and divide it among 6 salad plates.

3 Place 1 slice of grilled salmon on each salad. Spoon the remaining dressing over the salmon and serve immediately.

Wine Suggestion - This salad goes equally well with the Byron Vineyard and Winery Chardonnay or Pinot Noir.

CEDAR MOUNTAIN WINERY

Cedar Mountain Winery was established in the Livermore Valley in 1990 by Linda and Earl Ault. After buying Blanche's Vineyard in 1988, the Aults grafted the four-year-old Chenin Blanc vineyard to a mixture of Chardonnay and Cabernet Sauvignon in 1989.

Cedar Mountain Winery combines the creative interests of Linda and Earl: wine, food and art. Earl is an accomplished sculptor, watercolorist and large-format photographer. Linda is a recognized gourmet chef and caterer. Together they manage the farming activities and operate the winery with Earl as the winemaker.

The Aults believe that quality wines begin with the grapes in the vineyard. They specialize in Livermore grown and produced wines, whose full potential is realized with fine oak cooperage. They produce estate Chardonnay and Cabernet Sauvignon, as well as Livermore Valley Sauvignon Blanc.

✗ *This may sound like an unlikely combination of ingredients, but graphically it illustrates the diversity of the Central Coast: the sea, the soil and the farm. The salad makes a lovely first course or main dish when dining al fresco is in order.*

✵

ARTICHOKE AND CALAMARI SALAD
WITH WARM GOAT CHEESE DRESSING
4 portions

8 whole squid, cleaned, each about 3-inches long
1/2 cup hearts of palm, cut into 1/4-inch slices
1/4 cup roasted red pepper, peeled, and cut into small dice
6 tablespoons olive oil
1 tablespoon Cedar Mountain Winery's Blanches
    Vineyard herbed-wine vinegar
1 teaspoon chopped fresh chervil leaves, or Italian parsley
Salt and freshly ground black pepper, to taste
4 large artichoke bottoms, fresh or canned
1 ounce fresh goat cheese
4 cups lightly packed assorted greens, torn into bite size pieces

1 Rinse the squid under cold running water until they are thoroughly cleaned. Cook them in boiling water for 5 minutes. Immediately rinse the squid under cold running water to stop the cooking. Slice the bodies into 1/4 inch round slices. Leave the tentacles whole.

2 In a small bowl combine the squid, hearts of palm, roasted peppers, 3 tablespoons of the olive oil, vinegar, chervil, salt and pepper. Toss the ingredients together lightly, and refrigerate for 1 hour.

3   Meanwhile, brush the artichoke bottoms with 1 tablespoon of olive oil and grill or broil until lightly browned on each side. Set aside and let cool to room temperature.

4   Combine the goat cheese with the remaining 2 tablespoons olive oil in a microwave-safe bowl and mix well. More olive oil may be needed to get the desired consistency. Microwave the cheese mixture for about 1 minute on medium power, until the cheese mixture is warm but not hot. Be very careful not to overcook.

5   Arrange 1 cup of the greens on each salad plate and top each with 1 artichoke bottom. Fill each artichoke with the squid mixture, dividing it evenly. Drizzle some warm goat cheese dressing over each salad and serve immediately.

Wine Suggestion - Enjoy this salad with Cedar Mountain Winery Sauvignon Blanc.

LIVERMORE VALLEY CELLARS

In 1978 Livermore Valley cellars produced its first vintage as a winery, however, Chris and Beverly Lagiss' involvement in the Livermore Valley wine industry started some twenty years prior. While working at the Livermore labs during the mid-fifties, Chris decided he wanted a place in the country to raise his family. As a result he purchased a 34-acre parcel of land, complete with a vineyard.

After 20 years of grape growing and home winemaking, Chris realized the uniqueness of his vineyard and the quality flavor of his grapes. Based on the philosophy that you can't make good wine unless you have good grapes, the next logical step was to start a winery. Until 1990 only estate bottles of wine were produced, but since then they have started purchasing small, choice lots of grapes from local growers who share their winegrowing philosophy.

Today Livermore Valley Cellars produces 1,000 to 3,000 cases of wine a year and is still growing strong.

✻ *This is a quick and easy hors d'oeuvre that takes about five minutes to prepare. It is a guaranteed crowd pleaser. At Christmas time surround the spread with sprigs of freshly cut herbs to create an aromatic and tasty wreath effect.*

❀

LIVERMORE VALLEY CELLARS FETA CHEESE SPREAD WITH SUN-DRIED TOMATOES AND FRESH HERBS
2 cups

> 1 ounce dried tomatoes
> 1 cup Livermore Valley Cellars Chardonnay
> 8 ounces Feta cheese, coarsely crumbled
> 8 ounces cream cheese or goat cheese, at room
>   temperature
> 6 tablespoons unsalted butter, at room temperature
> 1 clove finely minced garlic
> 3 tablespoons finely minced fresh herbs, any combination

1   Place the dried tomatoes in the wine to soften them, about 1 hour. Drain the wine and discard. Set the tomatoes aside.

2   Place the Feta, cream cheese and butter in the bowl of a food processor fitted with a steel blade, and process until smooth. Add the tomatoes, garlic and herbs. Process until the mixture is almost smooth, but you can still see bits of herbs and tomato.

3   Transfer the mixture to a serving bowl and serve on crackers or thinly sliced French baguettes.

Wine Suggestion - Serve with Livermore Valley Cellars Chardonnay.

MAISON DEUTZ SPARKLING WINERY

In 1981 Andre Lallier-Deutz, the fifth generation proprietor and Chef de Caves of Champagne Deutz of France, discovered what he had been looking for to establish his California Methode Champenoise operation. In Arroyo Grande he found the combination of rolling, well-drained hills with chalky limestone soils in a very cool climate. These were planted to the Pinot Blanc, Pinot Noir, and Chardonnay grape varieties. Similar conditions prevail in the town of Ay, France, where Champagne Deutz has just celebrated their 150th Anniversary.

The winemaking philosophy at Maison Deutz is to use the wonderful, cool-climate fruit and state-of-the-art equipment in combination with traditional French techniques to achieve the perfect balance of fruit and complexity. The coastal valley location is superb for the production of sparkling wine of great depth and finesse, with an ideal expression of fruit.

�֍This tasty appetizer spread is delicious on English biscuits, such as Carr's Table Water, or toasted country French bread. The complexity and slight saltiness of the Bleu cheese is a delightful complement to the sparkling wine. The proportions are three-parts cream cheese to one-part Bleu cheese, so scaling-up the recipe is a breeze.

❦

DEUTZ BLEU CHEESE SPREAD
2 cups

4 ounces Bleu cheese, crumbled, at room temperature
12 ounces cream cheese, at room temperature
2 tablespoons Maison Deutz Sparkling Wine
1/2 cup finely chopped pecan pieces
3 tablespoons fresh chives, finely chopped
1 teaspoon freshly ground black pepper

1 In a food processor fitted with a steel blade, or in a blender, mix the Bleu cheese, cream cheese and sparkling wine until smooth. Transfer the mixture to a bowl.

2 Add the pecans, chives and pepper and stir to mix well. Adjust seasonings to taste. Cover and refrigerate until ready to use. This will keep in the refrigerator for 3 days.

Wine Suggestion - Serve with Maison Deutz Sparkling Wine.

MARTIN BROTHERS WINERY

Martin Brothers Winery is well-known for its Italian-style wines, especially Nebbiolo — a classic, high-quality grape from the Piedmont region of Italy — grown and produced here since 1981.

Other classic wines include Cabernet Etrusco, a blend of Cabernet Sauvignon and Sangiovese, several light and festive white wines, and a selection of distinctive dessert wines. All of the Martin Brothers wines come in Italiante packaging that includes imported bottles and labels featuring Italian art.

✖ *The herbal spice of Martin Brothers Nebbiolo is a perfect match for the pepper and garlic flavors of this Mediterranean-inspired dish. For a lighter combination use less garlic and pair with a Martin Brothers Chardonnay. This original recipe is from Mary Baker and was featured in Bon Appetit.*

PASO ROBLES PRAWN GAZPACHO
8 portions

> 2 to 3 cloves finely minced garlic
> 1/4 cup olive oil
> 1/4 cup freshly squeezed lemon juice
> 1/4 cup red wine vinegar
> 1 pound cooked prawns or large shrimp, peeled
>   and deveined
> 2 cups canned tomato juice
> 3 cucumbers, peeled and coarsely chopped
> 2 green bell peppers, cored, seeded and coarsely
>   chopped
> 2 red bell peppers, cored, seeded and coarsely
>   chopped
> 6 small jalapeno peppers, seeded and coarsely
>   chopped
> 12 Roma tomatoes, seeded and coarsely chopped
> 1 bunch fresh cilantro leaves
> 2 bunches green onions, trimmed and chopped
> Freshly ground black pepper, to taste
> 1 lemon, cut into 8 wedges, for garnish

1   In a mixing bowl whisk together the garlic, olive oil, lemon juice and red wine vinegar. Add the prawns. Cover the mixture and refrigerate for 1 hour.

2   Puree all the vegetables in small batches in a blender or food processor, adding the tomato juice gradually to keep the blades from clogging. Do not puree completely; the gazpacho should retain some of its crunch.

3   Stir in the prawn mixture and season with black pepper. Cover and chill for at least 4 hours.

4   When you are ready to serve, stir the soup, taste and correct seasonings. Ladle it into chilled soup bowls or mugs. Garnish with lemon wedges and serve.

Wine Suggestion - Serve with Martin Brothers Nebbiolo or Martin Brothers Chardonnay.

PEACHY CANYON WINERY

Peachy Canyon wines are perennially at or near the top of most rankings of California's Zinfandels. The winery is located just west of Paso Robles in Peachy Canyon, which was named for an old horse thief named Peachy.

A small winery that produces about two thousand cases a year, Peachy Canyon specializes in full-bodied Zinfandels and Cabernet Sauvignons and will be releasing a Merlot in the near future. The winery plans to gradually increase in size as their estate-planted vineyard begins to bear fruit.

Built in 1989 on Doug and Nancy Beckett's property, the 7,000 square-foot winery can produce up to 5,000 cases per year.

✖*This appetizer is a good way to use salmon "the second time around" and improves in the refrigerator, making it a perfect do ahead hors d'oeuvre. Using grilled salmon adds a nice smoky nuance that complements the Zinfandel.*

CREAMY SALMON PATÉ
2 cups

1 1/4 cups (14 3/4 ounce) cooked or canned salmon
1 package (8 ounces) cream cheese
1 teaspoon Worcestershire sauce
1 package (0.4 ounce) ranch-style dry mix dressing
1 tablespoon dehydrated minced onion
1 tablespoon freshly squeezed lemon juice
1 garlic clove, finely minced
1/4 teaspoon dry mustard
1 tablespoon finely chopped sun-dried tomato, in oil
    (optional)
1 cup fresh Italian parsley, finely chopped

1 Line a 2 to 3 cup mold or bowl with plastic wrap. Set aside.

2 Drain the salmon (if using canned) and remove all skin, bones and dark meat. Set aside.

3 In a mixing bowl, stir together the cream cheese, Worcestershire sauce, dry dressing mix, minced onion, lemon juice, garlic, mustard and sun-dried tomato, if using. Stir in the salmon and parsley.

4   Transfer the salmon mixture to the mold and press it in firmly, smoothing the top. Cover and chill at least 2 hours, or overnight.

5   To serve, invert mold on a serving platter and remove plastic wrap. Surround with fresh vegetables, sliced French bread and crackers.

Wine Suggestion - Serve with Peachy Canyon Winery Zinfandel or Cabernet Sauvignon.

Retzlaff Vineyards

All of the 3,000 cases of wine at Retzlaff Vineyards is bottled on the estate, where it stays until it is sold. Bob and Gloria Retzlaff bought the property and planted the vineyard in virgin soil about fifteen years ago. They opened the winery seven years ago. A family of wine enthusiasts, Bob is the winemaker and spent his professional career as a research chemist at the University of California. Their youngest son, Noah, is the assistant winemaker, having just returned from a ten-month stay in Bordeaux.

Retzlaff wines have won gold medals at all of the major California wine competitions, the most prestigious being the double gold at the California State Fair in 1991. Only nine wineries a year receive this honor.

The flavors of the wine come from the soil, and from that soil, the subtle elegance of the Retzlaff wine is created. The supple and silky smooth texture make them drinkable at an early age, while the rich, long finish supports their longevity.

✗*A hearty one-dish meal for a cold winter night. Serve it with crusty garlic bread and a green salad.*

COUNTRY PEA SOUP
6 portions

1 pound dried green or yellow split peas
8 cups hot water
1/4 cup Retzlaff Chardonnay
1 meaty ham bone, or 2 smoked ham hocks
3 garlic cloves, finely minced
1 onion, coarsely chopped
2 potatoes, coarsely chopped
3 carrots, peeled and coarsely chopped
Handful of parsley, finely chopped
Salt and freshly ground black pepper, to taste
Pinch of cayenne pepper
1 bay leaf
2 whole cloves

1 Rinse the split peas in a strainer. Then combine them with the water and Chardonnay in a large soup pot. Bring to a boil.

2 Add all the remaining ingredients, reduce the heat to medium-low and simmer partially covered, stirring occasionally, for 1 1/2 to 2 hours.

3 Remove the soup from the heat. Remove the ham bone and shred the meat from the bone, removing any excess fat. Return the meat to the soup. Taste and correct seasonings, and serve.

Wine Suggestion - Serve with Retzlaff Chardonnay.

SANFORD WINERY

Sanford Wines are currently produced from grapes grown in several well-established vineyards in Santa Barbara County. Each of these vineyards benefits from the unique topography of the country's east-west running mountains and valleys, which are open to the cooling influence of prevailing westerly winds. This setting is ideal for grapes requiring a cool growing climate.

The Sanford Winery was established in 1981 by Richard and Thekla Sanford. The winemaking at Sanford, with winemaker Bruno D'Alfonso at the helm, is traditional in its approach. White wine fermentation takes place in French oak barrels, and a portion of the Sauvignon Blanc is fermented in open-top stainless steel tanks. The annual production at Sanford Winery is 30,000 cases, which includes Chardonnay, Sauvignon Blanc, Pinot Noir and Pinot Noir-Vin Gris.

Each year artist Sebastian Titus is commissioned to paint a series of wildflowers native to the Santa Barbara area. These paintings, a different one for each variety and vintage, are reproduced in full color for the distinctive Sanford labels.

❋This dish was created by wine and food authority Shirley Sarvis of San Francisco. The prosciutto is intended to cling to the pork as the skewer is lifted to be eaten. The prosciutto should be of a subdued variety — lean, moist and fully spiced, not salty or dry. Garnish the serving trays with fresh sage leaves.

❦

SAGE PROSCUITTO PORK
48 appetizers

1 pound fresh, boneless pork loin, trimmed of all fat
Salt and freshly ground black pepper, to taste
2 1/2 tablespoons minced fresh sage leaves, or 4 tea-
spoons ground dry sage
Small amount of light tasting olive oil
2 ounces moist, lean prosciutto, cut into finely
julienned strips

1   Slice the pork very thinly against the grain. Place the pork in a single layer between 2 sheets of plastic wrap. Pat gently with a meat pounder or rolling pin to a thickness of 1/8-inch. Cut each slice lengthwise into 1-inch strips.

2   Season the strips with salt then generously with black pepper and sage. Cover with plastic wrap and let stand for 1 hour.

3   Thread on small skewers, flattening the meat to make individual appetizers. Brush both sides lightly with the olive oil.

4   Heat a griddle over high heat and place the pork strips on it. Grill the meat until it is golden brown and juicy inside. Arrange on a serving platter and sprinkle with the prosciutto. Serve immediately.

Wine Suggestion - Serve with Sanford Winery Sauvignon Blanc.

Santa Barbara Winery

In 1962 Pierre Lafond reestablished Santa Barbara County's winemaking tradition by founding Santa Barbara Winery. Much later, in 1981, Lafond invited Bruce McGuire, a winemaker for R&J Cook in the Sacramento delta, to take over the winemaking operation at Santa Barbara Winery. Since then Bruce has crafted award-winning wines and has earned a reputation as one of California's top winemakers.

McGuire's winemaking philosophy holds that the quality and the integrity of the wines are linked to what happens in the field. The long list of wines produced at Santa Barbara Winery are vibrant and fruity, capturing the essence of grapes as they taste in the vineyard.

✷*Bruce spends most Saturday mornings shopping at Santa Barbara's Farmers' Market where he finds most of the ingredients for this recipe. He gets his mushrooms from David Mountain, of Mountain Mushrooms.*

BRUCE MCGUIRE'S GRILLED STUFFED MUSHROOMS
4 portions

4 giant or 8 (2-3") fresh shiitake or portobello mushrooms
1 clove minced garlic or 1 minced shallot
6 to 8 marinated sun dried tomatoes, minced
1/2 cup grated Gruyere cheese
2 tablespoons Santa Barbara Winery Pinot Noir
1 tablespoon each, minced fresh thyme, basil,
*   epazote*, and oregano*
*1/4 cup chopped pecans, or toasted pine nuts***
Salt and pepper, to taste
Extra virgin olive oil

* If unavailable, the recipe can be prepared without epazote. Epazote is an herb frequently used in Mexican cooking and is not generally available in stores. It is a perennial that grows readily in home gardens and is used fresh, never dried.

** To toast pine nuts, preheat the oven to 350ºF. Spread out the nuts on a baking sheet and place them in the oven. Bake for 3 to 5 minutes. Check after 3 minutes. They pass from toasted to burned in seconds.

1   Remove the stems from the mushrooms and grate or mince the stems.

2   In a small bowl combine the stems, garlic, sun-dried tomatoes, Gruyere cheese, Pinot Noir, herbs and nuts.

3   Season the stuffing to taste with the salt and pepper. (If the sun-dried tomatoes are salty, no additional salt may be needed.)

4   Brush the mushroom caps with the olive oil and mound the stuffing inside.

5   Grill or broil until the cheese starts to melt, about 10 minutes.

Wine Suggestion - Serve with Santa Barbara Winery Pinot Noir.

TWIN HILLS WINERY

Twin Hills Winery was established as a commercial winery in 1982. The original proprietor developed and implemented environmentally conscious methods to minimize the use of all chemicals in the farming and the winemaking process. The current owners, Caroline Scott and Glenn Reid, are proud of this philosophy and believe this practice is important to the quality of its products. It is their intent to continue in the founder's practices in the production of "natural wines."

The pride and joy of Twin Hills Winery is its California Dry Sherry, made from Palomino grapes, using an ancient traditional Spanish "solera" technique — most Californian sherries are artificially baked rather than naturally fermented. Other estate-bottled wines include 100 percent varietal Chardonnay, Cabernet Sauvignon and Zinfandel. They also utilize Zinfandel grapes in the making of fruity, pleasant, "easy to drink" wines such as Beaujolais, Rose and White Zinfandel.

✗Spanish Pisto is an excellent addition to an assortment of tapas. It is perfect to make at the end of summer when the garden is overflowing with squash, peppers and tomatoes. It is healthy and delicious, good hot or cold, and freezes beautifully.

❈

SPANISH PISTO DIP
2 cups

3 tablespoons olive oil
1 1/2 cups coarsely chopped onions
2 small zucchini, scrubbed and cut into 1/4-inch cubes
1 large green bell pepper, cored, seeded and coarsely chopped
2 medium-sized tomatoes, peeled, seeded and coarsely chopped
1/2 teaspoon salt

1   In a large, heavy skillet heat the olive oil over high heat until a light haze forms above it. Add all the vegetables and the salt and stir together.

2   Reduce the heat to low and simmer, uncovered for 45 minutes, stirring occasionally to keep the vegetables from sticking to the pan. The Pisto is done when all the excess liquid is cooked away, and the vegetables are tender.

3   Transfer the mixture to a serving bowl and surround with bread, crackers and raw vegetables.

Wine Suggestion - A perfect appetizer with a chilled James J. Private Reserve California Dry Sherry from Twin Hills Winery.

WILD HORSE WINERY & VINEYARDS

Wild Horse Winery and Vineyards is situated on a beautiful mesa above the Salinas River. It boasts panoramic views of the Santa Lucia mountain range through which evening fog drifts from Morro Bay. This unique setting provides the perfect growing conditions for vinifera grapes.

The name Wild Horse and Ken Volk have been synonymous since 1986, when the first release of his Pinot Noir put Wild Horse on the map. Wild Horse has since gone on to garner national and international acclaim as a high-quality, premium-wine institution.

At 35,000 cases, Wild Horse is committed to traditional winemaking techniques, excellence and value to the consumer and a long-term pledge to the superb wines of the central coast.

✻*This simply wonderful soup is delicious with corn bread and a tossed salad.*

✿

BLACK BEAN SOUP
6 to 8 portions

1 pound black beans
1 onion, peeled and chopped
1 medium carrot, peeled and chopped
1 stalk celery, chopped
6 cloves garlic, finely minced
1 ham bone or 1 cup ham skin and scraps
2 to 3 quarts chicken stock or water
1 1/2 tablespoons ground cumin
2 tablespoons Ancho chili powder
1/2 cup sour cream
2 tablespoons milk
Salt, to taste
1/2 cup fresh tomato salsa

1 Rinse and sort the beans, discarding any stones or discolored beans. Put the beans, onion, carrot, celery, garlic, ham bone and chicken stock to cover in a large heavy pot. Bring to a boil and skim off any scum that rises to the surface. Simmer slowly, loosely covered, until the beans are tender, about 2 hours. Add more stock if the level falls below the surface of the beans and stir often to prevent sticking and to ensure that the beans cook evenly.

2 When the beans are cooked, puree them in a food processor. Mix the bean puree with the cumin and chili powder.

3   Mix the sour cream and milk until smooth.

4   Heat the bean puree, adding more stock to get a consistency that will pour out of a ladle like thin hot cereal. Season with salt and pour into warm soup bowls. Drizzle the sour cream over each serving and put salsa in the center.

Wine Suggestion - This Black Bean Soup is delicious with a Wild Horse red wine — Merlot, Pinot Noir or Cabernet Sauvignon.

CHEF'S SELECTION

✗*This unique dish was the result of a collaborative effort between my colleague and long-time friend Don Reynolds and myself trying to create something unusual for the annual Sea Fare event at the Olde Port Inn, where caterers and restaurateurs pair with wineries to match their food with wine.*

It was our desire to create something that would work with Pinot Noir, yet not overpower the other seafood dishes. Much to our happiness, it was a huge success. People really liked their "walking tacos."

ORIENTAL SALMON SALAD HAND ROLLS
Makes 12 appetizer portions (to be eaten with your hands)

Salmon
1/2 cup plus 2 tablespoons peanut oil
1 handful rice stick noodles
1/4 pound salmon fillet, skinned, pin-boned and cut
    in 3/4 inch squares
1 tablespoon ginger, finely chopped
1/2 teaspoon Tommy Tang's Seasoning (optional)
1/2 teaspoon red pepper flakes
1/2 teaspoon Chinese five-spice powder
1 splash Wild Horse Pinot Noir
4 shiitake mushrooms, soaked if dried, stems removed
    and julienned
4 mushrooms, julienned
3 green onions, sliced diagonally
2 tablespoons grated daikon radish
2 tablespoons fresh basil leaves, cut in chiffonade
2 tablespoons fresh mint leaves, cut in chiffonade
12 butter lettuce leaves, separated and left whole
12 whole mint leaves for garnish

Dressing
3 tablespoons hoisin sauce
1 teaspoon dark sesame oil
2 tablespoons pecans, toasted and finely chopped
2 tablespoons sesame seeds, toasted
2 tablespoons tangerine or orange juice
2 tablespoons peanut oil

To prepare salmon

1 Heat 1/2 cup peanut oil in wok until very hot. Add noodles in small batches and cook until noodles puff. Remove immediately to paper towels and set aside. Discard used oil.

2 Toss the salmon with the ginger, Tommy Tang's Seasoning, red pepper flakes and Chinese five-spice powder. Reheat wok. Add 1 tablespoon peanut oil, when oil starts to smoke add the salmon mixture and stir-fry until barely done. Remove from wok and set aside in a large bowl. Deglaze wok with the Pinot Noir and add to the salmon.

3 To the hot wok add the remaining 1 tablespoon peanut oil, the shiitakes and the mushrooms. Stir-fry until barely wilted. Remove and add to salmon mixture.

To make the dressing

1 Add all dressing ingredients and mix until well combined. Set aside until ready to serve.

To serve

1 Toss salmon gently with dressing, green onions, grated daikon radish, basil leaves and mint leaves. Fill lettuce cups with noodles and top with salmon mixture. Garnish the top of each with a fresh mint leaf. Serve slightly warm or at room temperature.

To make as a salad

1 Substitute 8 cups baby organic lettuce for the butter lettuce and toss all ingredients together. Serves 6 salad portions.

Wine Suggestion - Serve with Pinot Noir.

$\mathscr{P}$ASTA · $\mathscr{P}$IZZA · $\mathscr{C}$REPES

CAREY CELLARS

Located three miles out of the Danish town of Solvang, Carey Cellars represents the romantic notion of what a winery should be: rustic, off the beaten path and highly individual. Known for making first-class wines, the winery is housed in an antique red barn surrounded by vineyards, while the tasting room is in the original farmhouse set in an oak-studded garden.

The Santa Ynez Valley is now known as one of the great wine-growing regions of California. Since 1987 Carey Cellars has been making award-winning Cabernets, Merlots, Chardonnays and Sauvignon Blancs. With an annual production of only 5,000 cases, winemaker Alison Green is able to focus intensely on her Carey vintages.

✂*Roma tomatoes, spinach and pine nuts come together with spaghettini to create a flavorful and satisfying meal. Serve this with crusty French bread and something decadent for dessert.*

✿

SPAGHETTINI CAREY
4 portions

1 pound spaghettini
4 tablespoons olive oil
1 cup chopped onion
3 cloves finely minced garlic (more, if you are a garlic lover)
6 Roma tomatoes, coarsely chopped
1 teaspoon salt
Freshly ground black pepper, to taste
2 cups fresh spinach leaves, washed and cut into strips
1/2 cup chopped parsley or basil
1/2 cup pine nuts or chopped walnuts
3/4 cup freshly grated Parmesan cheese

1 Bring a large pot of water to a boil. Add the pasta and cook at a rolling boil until tender. Drain, rinse under cold water and drizzle with 2 tablespoons of the olive oil. Set aside.

2 Heat the remaining olive oil in a large, heavy skillet. Add onion and garlic and sauté over medium heat until transparent, but not brown.

3 Increase heat to high, add tomatoes and cook for 2 minutes. Season generously with salt and pepper. Add spinach, parsley and nuts. Heat thoroughly but do not cook. The spinach should be just wilted.

4 Add pasta to the tomato mixture and toss well. Add cheese and toss gently once more. Serve immediately.

Wine Suggestion - Serve with Carey Cellars Pinot Noir or Carey Cellars Merlot.

EBERLE WINERY

Eberle Winery is located just outside of Paso Robles, part of California's Central Coast Region. The small boutique winery was constructed in a rustic style on top of a knoll and designed for efficient and scientific production of premium Cabernet Sauvignon and Chardonnay.

The elegant tasting room adjoins the winery with large windows that overlook the winemaking facility enabling the guest to view the operation. French doors open onto the patio with a picturesque view of the winery's estate vineyard. Once a month the tasting room is transformed into a beautiful dining room where guests are invited to an elaborate dinner presented by various chefs, and the fine quality of Eberle wines is showcased.

Gary Eberle is very fond of pasta. This is his version of the popular Fettucini Alfredo. A splendid complement to Eberle Chardonnay.

FETTUCINI CON PROSCIUTTO "CLUB EB"

4 to 6 portions

1/2 pound (2 sticks) unsalted butter
1 tablespoon plus 1 teaspoon olive oil
1/2 pound prosciutto, finely chopped
1/2 pound mild Italian sausage, casing removed
1 cup sliced mushrooms
6 cloves finely minced garlic
2 cups heavy or whipping cream
1 pound fettucini
1 cup freshly grated Parmesan cheese
1/4 cup chopped fresh cilantro

1 In a large skillet heat 1 tablespoon of the butter and 1 tablespoon of the olive oil over medium heat. Add the prosciutto and sausage. Sauté until the sausage is cooked, about 5 minutes. Drain off any excess fat.

2 Add the mushrooms and garlic and continue cooking for another 5 minutes until the mushrooms have given off their juices.

3 While the sausage mixture is cooking, melt the remaining butter over high heat in a medium sized saucepan, until the butter is frothy. Slowly add the cream and cook until the sauce comes to a rolling boil, stirring constantly. Continue cooking over medium heat without stirring until the sauce is reduced by one fourth and coats the back of a spoon, about 7 minutes.

4 Bring a large pot of water to a boil. Add the remaining 1 teaspoon of olive oil and salt to the water. Add fettucini and cook at a rolling boil until the fettucini is just tender.

5 Drain the pasta in a colander and then place in a heated serving-bowl. Add the cream sauce and toss gently. Add the sausage mixture, 1/2 of the Parmesan cheese and the cilantro and toss again. Serve immediately. Pass the remaining Parmesan at the table.

Wine Suggestion - Serve with the Eberle Winery Chardonnay.

GARLAND RANCH WINERY

Garland Ranch Winery is one of the Chateau Julien Winery labels. It is nestled comfortably in the bucolic ambiance of Central California's Carmel Valley. Since 1982, owners Robert and Patricia Brower have cultivated and nurtured award-winning wines, thus gaining a stellar reputation rivaled by few in the rich California wine traditions. The French country chateau is located just 15 minutes from Monterey.

Since its grand opening in June 1984, the winery has won more than 390 awards in both national and international competitions. The winery produces Merlot, private reserve Chardonnay, Semillion, Sauvignon Blanc, Johannisberg Riesling and Gewurztraminer, along with limited quantities of award-winning Cabernets.

✗Healthy and tasty is what people are searching for, and this fits the bill.

❦

GARLAND RANCH MARINARA SAUCE
8 portions

3 cans (28 ounces each) crushed tomatoes
10 small cloves garlic, finely minced
1 tablespoon freshly chopped Italian parsley
2 heaping teaspoons freshly chopped oregano
2 heaping teaspoons freshly chopped basil
1/2 teaspoon freshly chopped rosemary
1/2 teaspoon anise seed
1/2 teaspoon freshly ground black pepper
1/2 teaspoon celery salt
1 teaspoon sugar
1 1/4 cups Garland Ranch Merlot
1/2 cup finely chopped black and green olives
1 pound dried pasta — rigatoni, ravioli, ziti, or
    spaghetti
Freshly grated Parmesan for serving

1 Combine all of the recipe ingredients, except the pasta and cheese, in a non-reactive container, such as plastic or glass. Let stand for at least 12 hours in the refrigerator.

2 Pour the sauce into a large saucepan or Dutch oven. Simmer for 1 hour. Set aside until ready to serve.

3 Prepare your favorite pasta and toss with the sauce. Serve with cheese.

Wine Suggestion - A Garland Ranch Merlot rounds out this wholesome meal.

JANKRIS WINERY

JanKris is a family owned winery and vineyard located in the green, rolling hills of Templeton, in the heart of the Central Coast's renowned wine country. The quality of the grapes and wines produced on this picturesque estate reflect the pride of family participation. As a measure of this pride, proprietors Mark and Paula Gendron have named the vineyard for their two young daughters, January and Kristin, whose silhouettes appear on every label.

The entire family is involved in the dawn-to-dusk operations of the vineyard, keeping a vigilant eye on sun, storm and soil as the grapes mature. At harvest time they work side by side with the crew to hand-harvest the 46 acres, insuring that the fruit is picked at the peak of perfection. Grapes are then processed under the mastery of winemaker Michael Black, using techniques such as whole-berry fermentation to produce wines that are light, fruity and smooth, at an accessible price.

By selecting only premium varietals and nurturing them with skill, the family seeks to establish a heritage for these vineyards — a tradition of bringing nature's promise to its finest fruition. The knowledge and dedication of the JanKris family has already been rewarded with numerous medals for their estate-grown Merlot, Chardonnay and Zinfandel. Forthcoming harvest will include Pinot Gris and Syrah.

✂ *This sauce is reminiscent of a traditional Bolognese sauce with a boost of Zinfandel. It freezes very well and tastes good any time.*

❧

ANGEL HAIR PASTA WITH ZINFANDEL RAGU
6 portions

2 tablespoons unsalted butter
1 tablespoon extra virgin olive oil
1 clove finely minced garlic
1 cup finely chopped onion
1 carrot, peeled, and finely chopped
1 pound unseasoned meat loaf mix (beef, veal, pork),
*   or ground sirloin*
2 cans (14 1/2 ounces each) ready-cut peeled tomatoes
1/2 cup JanKris Zinfandel
Salt and freshly ground black pepper, to taste
1 teaspoon paprika
1/4 teaspoon freshly grated nutmeg
1/4 teaspoon red pepper flakes
1 tablespoon Italian (flat leaf) parsley, finely chopped
1/2 cup heavy or whipping cream
1 pound dried angel hair pasta or vermicelli
Freshly grated Parmesan cheese, for serving

1   Melt the butter and olive oil together in a flameproof casserole or Dutch oven over medium heat. Add the garlic, onion and carrot. Sauté, stirring occasionally until the vegetables are soft and tender, about 7 to 10 minutes.

2   Add the meat and continue cooking. Stir until the meat is browned. Add the tomatoes, Zinfandel, salt, pepper, paprika, nutmeg and red pepper flakes. Reduce the heat to low, stir the sauce, cover partially, and cook for 30 minutes.

3   Add the parsley and cream. Correct the seasonings and set aside while you boil the pasta. At this point the sauce may be refrigerated or frozen. The flavor improves over time.

4   Cook the vermicelli in boiling, salted water until it is al dente. Drain it and place it in a warmed pasta serving bowl. Spoon some of the sauce over the top and toss well. Spoon the remaining sauce over each portion and pass the cheese. Serve immediately.

Wine Suggestion - Serve with JanKris Zinfandel.

MERIDIAN VINEYARDS

Meridian Vineyards, located in Paso Robles, uses grapes from its estate vineyards as well as Chardonnay and Pinot Noir fruit from the cooler Edna Valley and Santa Barbara regions.

Winemaker Chuck Ortman, who played an active role in shaping the wine-making direction of more than twenty super-premium wineries in Napa and Sonoma Counties, has now established himself as one of the true superstars of the South-Central Coast region.

Meridian specializes in Chardonnay, Pinot Noir, Syrah and Cabernet Sauvignon.

✗ *The fresh thyme baked in the crust and added in the topping make this an especially toothsome pizza. Serve this casual dish when you feel like having a kitchen party.*

CARAMELIZED ONION, GOAT CHEESE AND WILD MUSHROOM PIZZA
4 portions

Thyme-Flavored Pizza Dough
1 cup warm water
1 package active dry yeast or 1/4 ounce compressed yeast
Pinch sugar
2 1/2 to 3 cups unbleached all-purpose flour
2 tablespoons olive oil
1 tablespoon minced fresh thyme
1/2 teaspoon salt

Pizza Topping
8 tablespoons (1 stick) unsalted butter
3 yellow sweet onions (Maui, Vidalia or Walla
*   Walla) sliced 1/4 inch thick*
2 tablespoons minced fresh thyme
1 tablespoon sherry or balsamic vinegar
Salt and freshly ground black pepper, to taste
8 ounces fresh wild mushrooms (chantrelles, porcini,
*   shiitake or button mushrooms, if wild mushrooms*
*   are unavailable), cleaned and sliced*
4 ounces fresh goat cheese, crumbled
5 sun-dried tomatoes in olive oil, drained and sliced

To make pizza dough

1 Combine the water, yeast, sugar and 1 1/2 cups of the flour in a large bowl. Mix well. Add the oil, thyme, salt and remaining flour. With your hands or a large wooden spoon, work the ingredients together until the dough holds its shape. (You may need less flour, so add the last half gradually.)

2 Place the dough on a lightly floured surface and knead until it is smooth and elastic, 5 minutes.

3 Transfer the dough to a lightly oiled 2-quart bowl. Cover the bowl with plastic wrap and let the dough rest until it has doubled in size, 1 hour.

4 When the dough has risen, place it on a lightly floured surface and roll it into a ball. Cover it with a towel and let rest for 15 to 20 minutes. The dough is now ready to be shaped, topped and cooked.

5 Thirty minutes before cooking, preheat the oven to 450°F. If you have a baking stone, place it on the lowest rack of the oven at this time.*

To prepare the topping

1 Heat 6 tablespoons of the butter in a large, heavy skillet. When it is hot, add the onions and 1 tablespoon of the thyme and sauté over medium-low heat, stirring occasionally, until slightly caramelized, about 45 minutes to 1 hour. Add the vinegar and cook 1 minute more. Season lightly with salt and pepper. Set aside to cool.

2 Heat the remaining 2 tablespoons butter in a skillet. When it is hot, add the mushrooms and sauté over high for 3 to 5 minutes. Sprinkle with pepper and reserve.

3 Lightly oil a pizza pan and sprinkle with cornmeal, or sprinkle cornmeal on a pizza peel. On a well floured surface, press the dough out to form a large circle. Transfer it to the prepared pizza pan or peel, and cover with the caramelized onions, leaving a 1/2-inch rim.

4 Spoon the cooked mushrooms evenly over the onions. Sprinkle the goat cheese over the mushrooms. Arrange the sun-dried tomatoes on top of the goat cheese, and top with the remaining 1 tablespoon thyme.

5 Carefully slide the pizza off the peel, onto the stone. Or place the pizza pan in the oven. Bake until the crust is brown and the top begins to brown, about 20 to 25 minutes.

You can bake the pizza in a pan or on the back of a baking sheet, but you won't get the true crisp crust of an Italian pizza without the stone...

> *Wine Suggestion - The sweetness of the onions complements the tropical components of Meridian Vineyards Santa Barbara County Chardonnay.*

MOSBY WINERY

What started out merely as a hobby is now a full-blown production. Bill and Jeri Mosby have been interested in wine since they first moved to Lompoc in 1959, and today they produce exceptional, award-winning wines.

In the past decade there has been a trend on the part of California wineries, including Vega and Mosby, to produce more "food friendly" wines. These wines would resemble the European style of wines thought to be more compatible with food, rather than the bigger, brawnier California wines of yesteryear.

The commitment of Mosby Winery is to produce lean, sleek wines that stand on their own yet provide a perfect partnership with food, as depicted on the label.

✗ *It seems too simple to be so good, but it is. Serve this tasty dish with crusty French bread, for sopping up juices, and a salad of tossed greens.*

FARFALLE PASTA WITH PACIFIC CLAMS
4 to 6 portions

> 2 pounds hard-shelled clams, preferably Pacific
>   clams*
> 1 tablespoon corn meal
> 1 tablespoon salt
> 1/4 cup extra virgin olive oil
> 4 garlic cloves, minced
> 1 can (28 ounces) Italian peeled tomatoes, drained
>   and chopped
> 1/2 cup jalapeno stuffed olives, quartered lengthwise**
> 2 tablespoons coarsely chopped fresh oregano
> 2 tablespoons coarsely chopped Italian flat-leaf parsley
> 1 cup dry Mosby Gewurztraminer
> 1 pound farfalle pasta (bow-tie noodles)

* When fresh clams are not available, use good quality canned whole clams (10 ounce can). Drain the clams and add them to the finished dish right before serving. Do not cook.

** If jalapeno stuffed olives are not available, use pitted green olives and add 1 to 2 tablespoons chopped, pickled jalapeno peppers.

1   Place the clams in a large bowl and cover them with cold water. Sprinkle with the cornmeal and salt. Let stand for 1 hour. Rinse and drain.

2   Heat the olive oil in a heavy non reactive skillet or saucepan over medium-high heat. Add the garlic and cook for about one minute.

3   Add the chopped tomatoes, olives, oregano and 1 tablespoon of the parsley. Cover and cook until tomatoes just begin to break down, about 3 to 5 minutes. Add the clams and the wine to the tomato sauce.

4   Cover the skillet and increase the heat to high and cook, shaking the pan occasionally to make sure each clam has contact with the heat, until the clams just open.

5   Transfer the clams to a bowl and keep warm.

6   Meanwhile, cook the pasta in boiling, salted water until cooked al dente.

7   Add pasta to the tomato mixture and toss over high heat to allow pasta to absorb some of the sauce, less than 1 minute.

8   Transfer the pasta to a large serving bowl and place clams all over the top of the pasta, being sure to pour any extra tomato sauce over the clams. Sprinkle with the remaining parsley. Serve immediately.

Wine Suggestion - Mosby Winery Gewurztraminer or Muscato di Fior D'Arancio
is the perfect accompaniment.

PESENTI WINERY

The Pesenti family planted their first Zinfandel grape vines in 1923. In 1934 they established Pesenti Winery. Pesenti Winery is the oldest original family winery in the Paso Robles Appellation.

In Italy the natives seldom use cheese on their seafood pastas, believing it is unnecessary for the flavor of the food. While this sentiment can be appreciated, one often finds very good seafood pastas in California with the addition of freshly grated Italian cheeses. Americans can never have too much of a good thing.

✗*A tossed mixed green salad and toasted garlic bread is all that is needed to accompany this delightful meal.*

PASTA SHELLS WITH CLAMS
4 portions

8 tablespoons unsalted butter
8 cloves garlic, finely minced
1/2 cup Pesenti Chablis
2 cans (10 ounces) whole baby chowder clams with liquid
1/4 teaspoon red pepper flakes
12 ounces large pasta shells
3 tablespoons Italian parsley, finely chopped
Salt and freshly ground black pepper, to taste
1 cup freshly grated Parmesan cheese (optional)

1 Heat the butter in a deep, heavy skillet. Add the garlic and cook over medium heat until the garlic is fragrant but not brown, about 3 minutes.

2 Add the wine, clam liquid from 1 can of clams, red pepper flakes, and simmer for 5 to 6 minutes. Set aside. (Discard the liquid from the other can of clams.)

3 Meanwhile, boil the pasta shells as directed on the package and drain well.

4 Reheat the sauce, if it has cooled. Add the clams and heat gently; clams should not overcook or they will become tough.

5 Add the shells to the sauce and toss them together to mix well. Season to taste with the salt, pepper and one half cup of the Parmesan and serve hot. Pass the remaining Parmesan cheese, if you like.

Wine Suggestion - This dish is delicious with Pesenti's Grey Riesling or Sauvignon Blanc.

THOMAS KRUSE WINERY

The Thomas Kruse Winery is a small winery that produces dry table wines and a limited amount of sparkling wine, mostly around the holiday season.

Owner and winemaker Thomas Kruse handles most of the production by himself, but he solicits help from the outside during the harvest. Tom is known for his special wines, namely Gilroy Red and Gilroy White, both of which are extremely dry table wines.

Located on Highway 152 at Hecker Pass Road, the Thomas Kruse Winery is open seven days a week from 12 to 5 p.m. Picnic facilities are available for small groups.

✄ *Tom says of his recipe, "You'll like it!" We certainly did. Garlic does amazing things — in this recipe it adds a velvety richness and depth of flavor. It is good for you too.*

PASTA WITH PRAWNS
6 portions

1 bottle (12 ounces) Atlantic brand clam juice
8 tablespoons (1 stick) unsalted butter
16 cloves garlic, sliced tissue thin
3 pounds medium prawns or shrimp, peeled and deveined
1 1/2 teaspoons Tabasco sauce
9 firm, ripe plum tomatoes, cut in 1/2-inch dice
1 bunch green onions, white bulb and all of the green cut in 3/8-inch slices
1 cup black olives, pitted and halved (Calamata or other imported preferred)
1 cup fresh or frozen corn kernels
1 pound imported dried linguini
Freshly grated Pecorino Romano cheese

1   Bring a large pot of water to a boil.

2   In a large, heavy skillet add the clam juice, butter and garlic. Simmer over very low heat for about 15 minutes.

3   Add the prawns and the Tabasco sauce to the skillet, increase the heat to medium and cook until the prawns just begin to turn pink.

4   Raise the heat to high and add the tomatoes, green onions, olives, and corn. Cover with a lid and cook for 4 minutes, until heated through.

5 While the sauce is cooking, add salt and linguini to the rapidly boiling water. Cook the linguini until just tender, about 12 minutes. Drain and toss with the sauce.

6 Transfer to a warmed serving bowl, and serve immediately with plenty of freshly grated Pecorino Romano.

Wine Suggestion - Serve with a tossed green salad and Thomas Kruse Chardonnay.

TOBIN JAMES CELLARS

Tobin James Cellars is a small winery specializing in food-compatible wines such as Zinfandel, Cabernet Sauvignon, Chardonnay, Merlot, Pinot Noir and late harvest Zinfandel. The winery produces only 6,000 cases a year to keep quality at its peak. This allows Toby time to visit Mexico at least three times a year.

Tobin "Toby" James Shumrick came to California in 1980 from an eastern winemaking family. He worked at Estrella, became assistant winemaker at Eberle, then winemaker at Peachy Canyon before starting his own label.

He built his 9,000-square-foot winery and tasting room in 1993 on Highway 46 East in the Paso Robles Appellation. The tasting room is a western style saloon showcasing a 100-year-old wooden tasting bar made by the Brunswick Company.

✖ *This dish is delicious with a salad of sliced red onion, oranges and avocado, dressed with seasoned rice vinegar and served with garlic bread.*

TOBY'S LINGUINE WITH PRAWNS
4 portions

1 pound prawns, shelled and deveined
Freshly squeezed juice of 1 lemon
9 ounces (1 package) fresh linguine
1 tablespoon olive oil
8 tablespoons (1 stick) unsalted butter
2 garlic cloves, finely minced
1 bay leaf
2 teaspoons finely minced fresh thyme
1 teaspoon freshly ground black pepper
3 tablespoons tomato paste
1/4 cup Tobin James Cellars Zinfandel
1 cup heavy or whipping cream
1/2 cup freshly grated Parmesan
1/2 cup plus 2 tablespoons Italian parsley, finely minced

1   Rinse the prawns, and squeeze the lemon juice over them. Toss well and set aside.

2   Bring a large pot of water to boil and cook the linguine according to package directions, being careful not to overcook the pasta. Drain the linguine and toss it with the olive oil. Set aside and keep warm.

3   In a medium saucepan melt the butter over medium heat. Add the garlic, bay leaf, thyme and pepper. Cook, stirring constantly for 2 minutes, until the garlic is fragrant. Add the tomato paste and Zinfandel and cook for 4 to 5 minutes. Add the cream, and bring the mixture back to a boil.

4   Add the prawns to the sauce and cook until they are pink. Remove the bay leaf and add 1/4 cup of the Parmesan and 1/2 cup of the parsley to the sauce. Taste and correct seasonings.

5   Spoon the prawn sauce over the linguine, sprinkle with the remaining parsley and serve immediately. Pass the remaining Parmesan cheese.

Wine Suggestion - Tobin James Cellars Zinfandel completes the meal.

WENTE BROS. WINERY

Wente Bros. Winery was founded in 1883. Since the early 1960's, the Wente family has been producing fine wines from their Arroyo Seco Vineyards in Monterey County. Today the fourth generation operates two historic wineries in the scenic Livermore Valley. The original winery is located on Tesla Road. A few miles away the Wente Bros. Sparkling Cellars features an elegant restaurant overlooking rolling vineyards.

This recipe comes to us by way of Kimball Jones, Executive Chef at Wente Bros. Restaurant. The color of the Beet Puree juxtaposed on the Saffron Cream is a feast for the eyes. This dish brings a festive touch of sunshine to the table.

FENNEL AND SMOKED SALMON RAVIOLI WITH SAFFRON CREAM AND BEET PUREE
4 portions

Smoked Salmon Filling
1 handful wood chips (apple, oak, etc.) and charcoal
*   for smoking*
8 ounces smoked salmon (directions follow)
Salt and freshly ground black pepper to taste
2 tablespoons extra virgin olive oil
1 medium fennel bulb, trimmed and cut into
*   1/4-inch dice, tops saved for garnish*
Beet greens (from the Beet Puree, below), washed,
*   stems removed and finely chopped*
1/2 cup (4 ounces) ricotta cheese
2 tablespoons dry jack cheese or Parmesan, finely grated
Freshly squeezed juice and zest of 1 lemon

Pasta
1 1/2 cups flour
2 large eggs

Saffron Cream
1/2 teaspoon saffron
1 cup Wente Bros. Chardonnay
1 tablespoon finely minced shallot
1 cup heavy or whipping cream
Salt and freshly ground white pepper, to taste
1 teaspoon freshly squeezed lemon juice
1 teaspoon freshly grated lemon zest

Beet Puree
1 medium beet, greens reserved for ravioli
3 tablespoons (or more as needed) heavy or whipping cream
1 tablespoon unsalted butter
Salt and freshly ground white pepper, to taste

To smoke the salmon

1 Soak the wood chips (apple, oak, etc.) in a bowl of water overnight.

2 Salt and pepper the salmon fillet. Make a small fire with the charcoal in a smoker or Weber Grill. When the fire has burned down to low embers put a handful of the soaked wood chips on the coals and place the salmon on the grill. Put the top on the smoker and cook for about 20 minutes or until the salmon is cooked through. Cool completely.

To make the filling

1 In a large skillet or sauté pan heat the olive oil over medium-high heat. Add the fennel and beet greens and sauté, stirring constantly until the fennel is almost tender, about 5 minutes. Remove from the heat and cool completely.

2 In a mixing bowl combine the reserved salmon, fennel mixture, ricotta, dry jack, lemon juice and zest. Mix gently, but thoroughly and add salt and pepper to taste. Set aside or refrigerate until ready to use.

To make the pasta

1 In the bowl of a food processor fitted with a steel blade, add the flour and eggs. Process until thoroughly combined. Turn the dough out onto a lightly floured surface and knead it until it has formed a round ball. Cover with a kitchen towel and let it rest for 30 minutes.

2 Divide the dough in half. Roll one piece slightly with a rolling pin. Flour the dough lightly on both sides. Roll the dough through the widest setting of a pasta machine. Fold the pasta in thirds and roll it through the machine again. Continue rolling the pasta through the machine, gradually making the opening smaller, until you have reached the second thinnest setting. It is now ready to be cut for ravioli. Repeat with the remaining piece of dough.

To make the ravioli

1 Lay a sheet of pasta dough on a lightly floured surface. Make 12 round balls with the salmon filling, and place them 4-inches apart on the pasta. Brush the pasta sheet with water around the filling to help seal the edges. Lay the other sheet of pasta on top and press down lightly.

2   Using a pastry crimper cut the dough into squares, making sure the filling is in the center of each square. Place the raviolis on a lightly floured tea towel and refrigerate or freeze until ready to cook.

To make the sauces

1   Combine the saffron, Chardonnay and shallots in a saucepan. Cook rapidly over high heat until reduced to 1/3 of the original volume. Add the cream and cook over medium heat until the mixture has reduced and thickened slightly, 3 to 5 minutes. Remove the pan from the heat. Pour the sauce through a sieve and add salt, pepper, lemon juice and zest. Taste and correct seasonings.

2   In a separate pan, boil the unpeeled beet in water until it is tender. Drain and peel the beet. Puree the beet in a blender and add the cream, butter, salt and white pepper. Adding more cream until it reaches a sauce consistency.

Final preparation and assembly

1   Bring a large pot of salted water to a boil. Drop in the ravioli and cook until they rise to the surface, 2 to 3 minutes. Drain.

2   To serve place 3 ravioli on each warmed plate. Spoon the Saffron Sauce over the top, and then drizzle the Beet Puree in a design over the sauce. Serve immediately.

Wine Suggestion - Serve a Wente Bros. Chardonnay to complement this meal
—Estate Grown, Riva Ranch or Herman Wente Reserve.

WINDEMERE WINES

"MacGregor" is a Scottish name. The Windemere refers to a small region in Scotland where the MacGregor clan originated. Although long since destroyed by numerous battles, the ancestral villages of Windemere linger forever in the hearts and souls of those still proudly bearing the MacGregor name.

Founded by Cathy MacGregor in 1985, the Windemere approach to winemaking is definitely California-style. It is winemaker Cathy MacGregor's personal goal to create deliciously fresh and fruity wines, delicately augmented — yet never overwhelmed by — French oak and malolactic fermentation.

Perhaps the flowing watercolor label art on each bottle of Windemere wine best expresses the preferred winemaking style. Windemere Winery strives for a full-spectrum of fruit flavors delivered in a naturally balanced and harmonious style.

✗These crepes have the distinction of being both light and rich; a balanced foil for the Chardonnay. The crepes can be assembled hours ahead and baked at the last minute — good for brunch, lunch or a light dinner.

✿

WINDEMERE SEAFOOD AND HERB CREPES
6 portions

Herb Crepe Batter
1 1/2 cups milk
4 eggs
1 1/8 cup pastry or unbleached all-purpose flour
1/2 teaspoon salt
1 teaspoon each: finely chopped fresh tarragon, dill,
    Italian parsley and chives
1 tablespoon unsalted butter, melted

Seafood Filling
2 tablespoons unsalted butter
1 clove garlic, finely minced
1 cup red bell pepper, seeded and cut in 1/4-inch dice
1 cup sliced mushrooms
Juice of 1 lemon
1 1/2 cups Windemere Chardonnay
1/2 pound red snapper fillet, pin-boned and cut into
    1-inch cubes
1/2 pound medium shrimp, peeled, deveined and cut
    in half lengthwise
1/2 cup sliced green onions
2/3 cup freshly grated Gruyere cheese

Windemere Wine Sauce
2 tablespoons unsalted butter
2 tablespoons flour
1 1/2 cups half-and-half
1/3 cup freshly grated Gruyere cheese
2 tablespoons freshly grated Parmesan cheese
1 tablespoon Dijon mustard
1 teaspoon freshly ground white pepper
1/4 teaspoon cayenne pepper
24 sprigs fresh cilantro, for garnish

To make the crepe batter

1   Combine the milk, eggs, pastry flour and salt in a mixing bowl. Whisk well, and then pour the batter through a fine-mesh sieve into another bowl. Let the batter rest for 1 hour at room temperature before cooking. Just before you cook the crepes, add the fresh herbs and butter.

2   Heat an 8-inch crepe pan or non-stick skillet over medium-high heat until very hot. Lower the heat to medium. Spray the pan with a non-stick cooking spray and pour in a scant 1/4 cup of the batter. Swirl the pan to form a crepe 8-inches in diameter. Cook until the first side is set, about 1 minute, then turn the crepe and cook on the other side for about 15 seconds. Remove the crepe from the pan and repeat the process, spraying the pan as needed. Stack the crepes, and when you are done, wrap them in plastic wrap. Set aside or refrigerate for longer storage, or freeze up to 1 month. Makes 12 crepes.

To make the seafood filling

1   In a large skillet melt the butter and sauté the garlic, red bell pepper and mushrooms over medium-high heat for 3 minutes. Add the lemon juice and wine and boil to reduce the liquid by one-fourth its volume. Add the red snapper and cook for 30 seconds, then add the shrimp and cook until the shrimp are barely pink. Remove the seafood and vegetable mixture from the liquid, and place it in a bowl. Reserve the liquid and set aside.

2   Into the bowl with the seafood, add the green onions and cheese and mix thoroughly. Using about 1/4 cup of the seafood filling, fill and roll each crepe into a cylinder and place in a buttered oven-proof 13 x 9 inch dish.

3   Place the dish in preheated 350°F. oven and bake for 15 to 20 minutes, while preparing the sauce.

To prepare the sauce

1   In a medium saucepan melt the butter over medium heat. Add the flour and stir until it forms a paste but do not let it brown. Add the reserved cooking liquid and the half-and-half and bring it to a boil, stirring constantly, until the sauce is thickened. Boil for 5 minutes. Remove from the heat and slowly add the Gruyere cheese, Parmesan cheese, Dijon mustard, white pepper and cayenne pepper. Stir until the cheese is melted. Taste and correct seasonings.

2   To serve, place 2 crepes on each warmed plate. Spoon some sauce over each crepe and garnish with sprigs of cilantro.

Wine Suggestion - Serve with Windemere Chardonnay.

CHEF'S SELECTION

✗*This lasagna is a lavish salute to spring. Full of tender asparagus spears, creamy goat cheese and lemon zest layered with paper-thin pasta sheets, this dish is sophisticated and deceptively light.*

Make this opulent dish the day before you serve for convenience and refrigerate. Notice that the asparagus is roasted in the oven. This method is so simple and delicious you will always want to do it this way. Serve with a tossed green salad.

❦

ASPARAGUS LASAGNA
8 portions

4 pound asparagus, washed and trimmed
2 tablespoons extra virgin olive oil
12 sheets (7 by 3 1/2 inch) instant (no boil) lasagna noodles
1/2 stick (1/4 cup) unsalted butter
1/4 cup unbleached all-purpose flour
1 1/2 cups chicken broth, preferably homemade
1/2 cup water
7 ounces mild goat cheese, such as Montrachet
1 teaspoon freshly grated lemon zest, or to taste
Salt, to taste
1 2/3 cups freshly grated Parmesan cheese
1/2 cup heavy cream

1 Preheat the oven to 500°F.

2 Cut the tips off of each asparagus spear and reserve them.

3 In each of two large shallow baking pans toss half of the asparagus spears with half of the oil, coating them well. Roast them in the preheated oven, shaking the pans every few minutes, for 5 to 10 minutes until they are crisp-tender. Let the asparagus cool, and cut into 1-inch lengths and reserve.

4 In a large bowl of cold water let the sheets of lasagna soak for 15 minutes or until they are softened.

5 In a saucepan melt the butter, add the flour and cook over medium heat, stirring, for 3 minutes. Add the broth and the water in a slow, steady stream, whisking. Simmer the mixture for 5 minutes. Add the goat cheese, lemon zest and salt to taste, whisking until the sauce is smooth. Set aside.

6   Drain the pasta well and arrange 3 sheets in a buttered 9 by 13 inch baking dish, and spread the sheets with one third the sauce. Top the sauce with 1/4 of the roasted asparagus, and sprinkle the asparagus with 1/3 cup of Parmesan. Continue to layer the pasta, sauce, asparagus and Parmesan in the same manner, ending with the pasta.

7   In a bowl beat the cream with a pinch of salt until it holds soft peaks. Arrange the reserved asparagus tips decoratively on the pasta, then spoon the cream over the top, spreading it with the back of a spoon, and sprinkle the remaining one third cup Parmesan on top.

8   Bake the lasagna in the middle of a preheated 400ºF. oven for 20 to 30 minutes, or until it is golden and bubbling. Let it stand for 10 minutes before serving.

Wine Suggestion - Serve this dish with a good white wine — a dry Johannisberg Riesling or Gewurztraminer.

$\mathcal{M}$ AIN $\mathcal{C}$ OURSES

ADELAIDA CELLARS

Adelaida Cellars was founded in 1981 by John and Andree Munch based upon the firm premise that fine wine delights in good conversation and leisurely meals, and all else is meaningless. A partnership was recently formed with Don and Elizabeth Van Steenwyk, who own three spectacular mountain ranches west of Paso Robles. As a result, Adelaida Cellars now sits high in the western hills, a dramatic setting with elevations ranging above 2,300 feet. The Pacific Ocean is a mere 14 miles in the distance, and everywhere you turn there is sun, bright stone, and wild herbs.

The winery takes its name from the old town of Adelaida, a mountain community that was once the farming hub of the district, an area that is now gaining prominence for its very special vineyards. The Adelaida label is from an original "maniere noir" engraving created by an English artist of questionable repute living in the south of France.

All grapes for Adelaida Cellars wines are hand picked into small bins. Chardonnay grapes are pressed whole cluster, with only the free-run juice retained. The Chardonnay is then barrel-fermented and aged on the lees for at least 10 months, with various vineyard lots blended to best advantage just prior to bottling. Cabernet Sauvignon and Zinfandel grapes also receive the delicate Adelaida treatment.

✘*Andree is from the Savoie region of France where the skiing is excellent and so is the food. This lovely gratin-style dish makes a terrific course on a chilly evening with a glass of Chardonnay.*

ANDREE'S ENDIVES AU JAMBON
6 portions

12 heads Belgian endive, all about the same size
2 tablespoons freshly squeezed lemon juice
1 cup water
2 tablespoons unsalted butter
2 tablespoons unbleached flour
Rich homemade chicken stock
3 ounces cream cheese or chevre
1/4 teaspoon each: Madras curry powder, nutmeg,
    and freshly ground white pepper
6 tablespoons freshly grated Parmesan cheese
12 very thin slices Cottage ham (1/2 pound)
12 very thin slices Gruyere cheese (1/2 pound)

1 Rinse the endives and remove any wilted outside leaves. Trim off 1/4-inch of the bottom of each endive, and using a small paring knife cut out a cone shaped section of the core. This eliminates any bitter or strong flavors, and helps the endives to cook evenly.

2   In a small bowl combine the lemon juice and the water. Dip each trimmed endive in the lemon water to prevent browning. Discard the lemon water.

3   Pour 1 1/2-inches of water into a large saucepan with a steamer basket. Add the endives, cover tightly and bring to a vigorous boil over high heat. Lower the heat to medium and steam the endives until tender without being mushy, about 10 to 15 minutes. Test the endives with the tip of a knife; they must be cooked through. Set aside to cool. Save the liquid from the steamer for the sauce.

Make the béchamel sauce

1   In a small saucepan melt the butter over medium heat. Add the flour and stir until it forms a paste, but do not let it brown. Measure the liquid from the steamer, and add enough chicken stock to make 1 1/2 cups. Pour this liquid into the butter-flour mixture and stir well to prevent any lumps from forming. When sauce is boiling and thickened, remove from heat. Stir in the cream cheese, the spices, and 4 tablespoons of the Parmesan. Set aside.

2   With your hands squeeze excess juice out of the endives. (This is important or the dish will be watery.) Place a slice of ham on a work surface, and lay a slice of Gruyere on top of the ham. Place 1 endive on one end and roll it up snugly in the ham and cheese. Continue rolling until all of the ingredients are used up. Place the rolled endives side by side, seam side down, in an oven proof dish.

3   Pour the béchamel over the endives, and sprinkle with the remaining 2 tablespoons Parmesan.

4   Bake the endives in a pre-heated 375°F. oven for 15 to 20 minutes, or until bubbling and golden on top. If you prefer a darker crust, run the dish under a very hot broiler until browned. Serve immediately.

Wine Suggestion - Enjoy with Adelaida Cellars Chardonnay.

AU BON CLIMAT WINERY

Jim Clendenen was born in Akron, Ohio, to gastronomically impoverished parents during the culinary dark ages of the American 1950s. Under the ownership of Jim Clendenen, Au Bon Climate has grown over the last ten years to 10,000 cases through careful re-investment from its own production. The company has cultivated an international reputation for its Pinot Noir, Chardonnay and Pinot Blanc.

In 1989, and again in 1990, Au Bon Climat was on Robert Parker's short list of best wineries in the world. Jim was selected by Oz Clarke in 1991 as one of 50 world-wide creators of "Modern Classic Wines." That same year Dan Berger of the *Los Angeles Times* selected Clendenen as number eight in his top-twenty California winemakers. Jim continues to get it right, and, in 1992, he went number one.

✗Lovely and strong are this dish's combination of flavor and color — the green of the salsa, the carrot rice, and the oak-grilled Ahi. It is simply excellent and healthy. Beware of the possible incendiary effects of the jalapeno seeds—leave them in at your own risk.

GRILLED AHI TUNA WITH ROASTED JALAPENO SALSA
6 portions

Sunday Rice for Sally
2 tablespoons canola oil
2 cups brown Basmati rice, rinsed and drained
2 cloves finely minced garlic
1 stick cinnamon
1 large chayote squash, cut into 1/2-inch dice
2 cups rich chicken stock, preferably homemade
2 cups carrot juice
Freshly squeezed juice of 1 lime
2 tablespoon fresh chives, finely chopped

Roasted Jalapeno Salsa
3 green jalapeno peppers
1 small clove garlic, finely minced
1/4 cup packed fresh cilantro leaves
2 tablespoons unseasoned rice vinegar
1/2 cup Au Bon Climat Chardonnay
1 cup very finely minced sweet onion (Vidalia, Walla Walla, or Maui)

Grilled Ahi
6 fresh (7 ounces each) Ahi steaks
Salt and freshly ground pepper, to taste

To make the rice

1 Heat the oil in a medium-sized Dutch oven or flameproof casserole over medium-high heat. Add the rice and sauté, stirring often, until all the rice kernels are golden-brown.

2 Add the garlic, cinnamon, diced chayote squash, and stir well. Pour in the chicken stock and carrot juice, stir and bring to a boil. Cover the casserole tightly and bake in a preheated 350ºF. oven for 40 minutes. Remove from the oven and tilt the lid at an angle to allow some steam to escape.

To make the salsa

1 Roast the jalapeno peppers over a gas flame until their skins are brown, not blackened, and remove from the heat. When the peppers are cool, slice in them in half, lengthwise, and scrape out the seeds.

2 In a blender combine the jalapenos, garlic, cilantro, rice vinegar and Chardonnay. Blend until smooth. Stir in the onion and place in a bowl in the refrigerator until ready to serve.

To cook the Ahi

1 Prepare an oak chip fire for grilling. Season the Ahi with salt and freshly ground black pepper. Grill the Ahi steaks over the hot oak coals until the Ahi is rare, or until the desired doneness is reached.

2 To serve, queeze the lime juice over the rice and sprinkle with the chives. Place the Ahi steaks on a platter with a small bowl of the salsa in the center. Pass the rice.

Wine Suggestion - Serve with Au Bon Climat Winery Chardonnay.

BABCOCK VINEYARDS

Babcock Vineyards is located ten miles inland on the western edge of the Santa Ynez Valley. Here the mountains run east and west, creating a marvelous coastal climate that draws cool ocean air into the valleys. This cool influence, coupled with good soils and gentle slopes, makes for an ideal vineyard site. Walt and Mona Babcock brought the 110-acre property in 1979. The first grapes were planted shortly thereafter.

The small harvest in 1982 showed great promise, and samples were delivered to various winemakers in the Santa Ynez Valley. Then in 1983 a few more tons were harvested. In 1984 Walt and his son Bryan decided to seize the opportunity and produce their own wines. So, in the month of June, construction on the winery began. One year later the first two gold medals for Babcock Vineyards were awarded to the 1984 Sauvignon Blanc.

Since then Bryan has accumulated numerous awards and accolades for his premium, hand-crafted wines. Currently Babcock Vineyards has acres planted with Chardonnay, Sauvignon Blanc, Riesling, Gewurztraminer, Syrah and Pinot Noir grapes. There are also a few acres of Walt's exotic lettuce, vegetables and fruit trees.

�֍ *This unusual and exotic combination of ingredients illustrates our Californian influence on what is often called "Fusion Cuisine."*

❧

MONA BABCOCK'S GINGERED PRAWNS
WITH SCALLION RISOTTO
4 portions

Scallion Risotto
2 tablespoons olive oil
1/4 cup finely minced red onion
1 bunch scallions, cleaned and sliced — white and
    green parts reserved separately
1 tablespoon finely minced garlic
1 cup Arborio rice
2 cups hot chicken stock, preferably homemade
1/4 teaspoon white pepper

Gingered Prawns
4 tablespoons rice wine vinegar
4 tablespoons minced pickled ginger
2 tablespoons minced pickled jalapeno peppers
4 teaspoons honey
1 cup water
1 tablespoon corn starch
4 teaspoons dark sesame oil

4 garlic cloves, finely minced
20 shrimp (16 to 20 per pound), shelled, cleaned,
*   and butterflied*
1 red bell pepper, cored, seeded and cut into fine julienne
*   strips*
4 tablespoons chopped cilantro

To make the risotto

1   In a large skillet with high sides, heat the olive oil over medium-high heat. Add the red onion, white part of the scallions and garlic and sauté until the onions are soft, about 5 minutes. Add the rice and sauté 3 minutes more.

2   Reduce the heat to medium-low and add 1/2 cup of the stock, stirring constantly until the stock is almost evaporated. Continue adding the stock 1/2 cup at a time until all the stock is used and the rice is tender, about 20 minutes. Stir in the white pepper and the green part of the scallions and taste and correct seasonings. Keep the risotto warm while preparing the shrimp.

To make the prawns

1   In a small bowl stir together the vinegar, ginger, jalapeno, honey, water and corn starch. Set aside.

2   In a large, heavy skillet heat the sesame oil over medium-high heat. Add the garlic and sauté 1 to 2 minutes, until the garlic is fragrant. Add the shrimp and stir-fry until the shrimp begin to turn pink. Pour in the jalapeno-sauce mixture and continue cooking until the sauce has thickened.

3   Place the Scallion Risotto on a large serving platter. Arrange the shrimp on the risotto, and pour the jalapeno sauce over all. Sprinkle the slivered red peppers over the shrimp and then top with the chopped cilantro.

Wine Suggestion - Serve with a slightly chilled Babcock Gewurztraminer.

B A I L E Y A N A   W I N E R Y
(FORMERLY TIFFANY HILL)

Tiffany's of New York objected to the use of the name Tiffany Hill, which was taken from the winery's address on Tiffany Ranch Road. As a result of this potential infringement, Tiffany Hill is now known as Baileyana.

Baileyana is a small, family owned estate producing only barrel-fermented Chardonnay in the classic Burgundian style. The wine derives its character from grapes grown on the extremely rocky terroir, supplemented with the award-winning fruit of its neighboring Paragon Vineyard.

✗Country Captain is a traditional dish that is a staple for entertaining in the southern United States. According to some sources the dish originated in India, and the word captain *is a corruption of the word* capon. *Regardless, it is a lovely dish for entertaining because it serves a crowd and can be made in advance and slowly reheated.*

COUNTRY CAPTAIN
12 portions

6 whole chicken breasts, split, rinsed and patted dry
12 chicken thighs, rinsed and patted dry
1 teaspoon salt
1 teaspoon freshly ground black pepper
4 tablespoons unsalted butter
2 medium onions, finely diced
1 green bell pepper, cored, seeded and finely diced
1/2 cup finely chopped fresh parsley
4 cloves garlic, finely minced
1 tablespoon curry powder
1 teaspoon dried thyme
1 cup Baileyana Chardonnay
2 large cans (28 ounces each) whole tomatoes with juice
1 bottle (14 ounces) ketchup
1 cup currants
1 pound blanched, toasted almonds
Chutney
Steamed rice

1   Preheat the oven to 350ºF.

2   Season the chicken pieces with the salt and pepper.

3   In a very large, heavy skillet heat 2 tablespoons of the butter over medium-high heat. When the foaming subsides, add the chicken in batches and brown well on all sides. As the chicken is browned, transfer the pieces to a very large oven-proof casserole or Dutch oven. Set aside.

4   After all the chicken is browned, drain off all the fat from the skillet. Return the skillet to the stove and add the remaining 2 tablespoons of butter. Add the onions, green pepper, parsley, garlic, curry powder and thyme. Sauté the mixture until the onions are wilted and the other vegetables are softened. Add the wine and cook until the liquid is reduced by 1/2 its volume.

5   Add the tomatoes, ketchup, and currants. Bring the mixture back to a boil, then pour over the chicken in the casserole.

6   Cover the casserole with a lid and bake for 45 minutes. Remove from the oven and skim off any fat that has accumulated on the top. Let the chicken rest for 15 minutes.

7   Serve with the blanched toasted almonds, chutney and steamed rice.

Wine Suggestion - The Baileyana Chardonnay with its bright fruit flavors is a delicious wine selection for this dish.

The Brander Vineyard

The planting of the Brander Vineyard to mainly Bordeaux varietals began in 1975. In 1977 the first harvest of Sauvignon Blanc grapes were taken to a neighboring winery where Fred Brander produced a wine so distinctive, it captured Santa Barbara county's first gold medal at the Los Angeles County Fair.

Since its inception the Brander Vineyard has been highly acclaimed as a top Sauvignon Blanc producer. Today, the winery produces an average of 8,000 cases of estate wine from its forty acres of vineyards in the Santa Ynez Valley. The principal wine is a Sauvignon Blanc (blended with Semillon), along with Bouchet (a blend of red Bordeaux varietals), and a small quantity of Chardonnay.

When you are lucky enough to get really fresh Pacific swordfish, the rule is to keep it simple. This recipe from Brian Moores, resident chef at Brander illustrates that less is truly more. Serve with lemon rice and a colorful vegetable melange.

Grilled Pacific Swordfish With Fennel Sauvignon Blanc Butter

6 portions

1 fennel bulb, trimmed
1/2 pound (2 sticks) unsalted butter, at room temperature
2 tablespoons Brander Tete de Cuvee Sauvignon Blanc
Salt and freshly ground black pepper, to taste
6 fresh swordfish steaks (8 ounces each)

1 Cut the fennel bulb in quarters and place in the bowl of a food processor fitted with a steel blade. Process until the fennel is finely chopped, but do not puree. Transfer the fennel to a mixing bowl.

2 Add the softened butter and Sauvignon Blanc to the fennel and mix well. Add salt and pepper to taste.

3 Shape the butter into a cylinder and wrap it in aluminum foil. Chill it in the refrigerator for at least 20 minutes.

4 Prepare hot coals for grilling.

5 Oil the grill, and cook the steaks over high heat, about 3 to 4 minutes per side. The steaks should be seared on the outside and just cooked through. Keep warm.

6 Remove the aluminum foil from the butter and slice the butter into 12 1/4-inch thick slices. Place 2 slices of fennel butter over each hot swordfish steak and serve immediately.

Wine Suggestion - Serve with Brander Vineyard Sauvignon Blanc.

BUTTONWOOD FARM WINERY

Several years ago Buttonwood Farm decided to produce small quantities of a few superb wines. In 1983 Buttonwood Farm vineyard was planted and later, in 1989, a small winery was built. There are now 33,000 vines planted over 39 acres, which is small in the world of wine but huge to them.

This is a beautiful vineyard, boasting a 360-degree view of the Santa Ynez Valley with a hilltop setting, light, rocky soil, which combined with careful watering, results in a very sparse-leaf canopy. This allows the grapes more exposure to the sun and air, intensifying its fruitiness.

This region is known for producing grapes that taste like fruit, not vegetables. Winemaker Michael Brown works to preserve that taste, and it shows through the finished bottle of wine. They released their first wine, a Sauvignon Blanc, in 1990. Two years later they introduced a Merlot. Everyone at Buttonwood Farms takes great pleasure in these wines and their work.

Serve with noodles, carrots and sweet-and-sour red cabbage.

MEDALLIONS OF PORK SOLVANG

2 portions

8 pork medallions (1/4-inch thick) from the tenderloin
Salt and freshly ground black pepper, to taste
2 heaping tablespoons corn meal
3 tablespoons olive oil
1 shallot, or 3 green onions, peeled and finely minced
1/2 cup finely chopped mushrooms
1/4 cup Buttonwood Sauvignon Blanc
1/2 cup chicken stock, preferably homemade
1 teaspoon cornstarch mixed with a little water
1 teaspoon each: finely minced fresh tarragon, finely minced fresh dill, minced fresh ginger, and soy sauce or tamari
Tabasco sauce, to taste
2 tablespoons sliced almonds or pine nuts

1 Salt and pepper the medallions. Dredge the pork medallions in the corn meal. Set aside.

2 Heat a large, heavy skillet over high heat and add the olive oil. When the oil is very hot add the pork medallions and sear on both sides, about 15 seconds, until just barely cooked. Remove the pork to a serving platter and keep warm.

3 In the same skillet, add the shallot and mushrooms and sauté for 5 minutes, or until tender. Add the Sauvignon Blanc, chicken stock, corn starch and water, tarragon, dill, ginger, soy sauce and Tabasco. Bring this to a boil and simmer for 4 minutes, stirring constantly. Taste and correct seasonings. Add the medallions and almonds and simmer to heat thoroughly. Serve immediately.

Variation: You may use this with any cut of fish, chicken or beef — always slice thinly. When using beef the sauce may be strengthened by adding additional vegetables and red wine.

Wine Suggestion - Serve with Buttonwood Sauvignon Blanc.

CASA DE FRUTA

Casa de Fruta blossomed from the roots of an immigrant Italian family. Since 1908 when the original ancestors planted the first orchards in the Pacheco Valley, Casa de Fruta has grown into a diversified operation encompassing retail stores, camping facilities, orchards and vineyard.

The vineyards planted in 1972 are located in the Pacheco Pass Viticultural Area. Warm days and cool nights contribute to the richly satisfying wines of Casa de Fruta. The vineyards produce Gewurztraminer, Johannisberg Riesling, Zinfandel, Chenin Blanc, Chardonnay and Muscat Hamberg varietals. In tribute to Casa de Fruta's long fruit growing tradition, they also produce apricot, plum, cherry, and pomegranate wines.

✗ *This wonderful chicken entree is perfect with rice or pasta.*

CHICKEN GEWURZTRAMINER
4 portions

2 tablespoons unsalted butter
2 tablespoons olive oil
1 chicken (1-1/2 to 3 pounds), well rinsed, cut into 8 serving pieces
Salt and freshly ground black pepper, to taste
2 cups tiny pearl onions, peeled, or 1 10-ounce bag frozen pearl onions
1/2 teaspoon sugar
1 tablespoon freshly squeezed lemon juice
1 9-ounce box frozen artichoke hearts
1/2 cup Casa de Fruta Gewurztraminer
1/2 cup chicken stock, preferably homemade
2 bay leaves

1 In a large, heavy skillet heat the butter and olive oil over medium high heat, until the butter stops foaming. Add the chicken pieces and brown well on all sides. Remove chicken from the skillet and place in a large casserole. Season the chicken to taste with the salt and pepper.

2 Add the onions and sugar to the skillet and cook until all the liquid has evaporated, and the onions are golden brown and caramelized, about 10 minutes. Place in the same baking dish with the chicken.

3 In the same skillet, add the lemon juice and sauté the artichoke hearts until they are cooked slightly. Add them to the baking dish with the chicken and onions.

4   Add the wine, chicken stock and bay leaves to the casserole and bake in a preheated 350°F. oven for 30 to 45 minutes, or until the chicken juices run clear when pierced with a fork.

Wine Suggestion - Serve with Casa de Fruta Gewurztraminer.

CASTORO CELLARS

A family owned and operated winery, Castoro Cellars has been producing great wines since 1983. Owners Bimmer and Niels Udsen have always felt that the Paso Robles appellation offered the finest grapes anywhere. Years of consistent gold-medal wines have attracted both national and international attention.

The dedicated team at Castoro Cellars is essential to the year to year consistency of the quality winemaking. The winery is a state-of-the-art facility, which is located in the northern Paso Robles appellation. The tasting room is located on Highway 46, west of Paso Robles, at its intersection with Bethel Road.

✗ *This relatively simple dish only looks like one that would take a long time to prepare. The flavors are subtle and elegant, and the aroma of the "pouches" being opened is divine. Serve with white rice or pasta.*

SEAFOOD POUCHES
4 portions

1 tablespoon minced fresh thyme
1/3 cup minced fresh tarragon
2 tablespoons minced fresh basil
Freshly ground black pepper, to taste
6 tablespoons unsalted butter, at room temperature
*2 medium leeks, white part only, rinsed and cut into
    thin 2-inch strips*
2 large carrots, cleaned and cut into thin 2-inch strips
1/2 pound Petrale sole, cut into 4 small fillets
1/2 pound bay scallops or sea scallops, cut in half
1/2 pound medium shrimp, peeled and deveined
Lemon half
4 tablespoons Castoro Chardonnay
Salt, to taste

1 Preheat the oven to 450°F.

2 In a small bowl mix together the thyme, tarragon, basil, pepper and butter. Set aside.

3 In a medium saucepan bring 1 quart of water to boil. When the water is boiling add salt and the leeks and carrots. Bring the water back to a boil, and blanch for 1 minute. Drain vegetables in a colander and set aside.

4   Lay out 4 strips of aluminum foil about 12-inches long. Divide half of the carrot-leek mixture evenly among the 4 pieces of foil. Arrange each piece of sole on top of the carrot-leek mixture. Top the fillets with the scallops and shrimp. Squeeze the lemon juice over and cover with the rest of the carrot-leek mixture. Add equal portions of the herb butter to each pouch. Add 1 tablespoon of Chardonnay to each pouch and salt to taste.

5   Seal the packets and set them on a baking sheet. Bake for 15 minutes. Remove the packets from the oven, set them on plates, and serve immediately.

Wine Suggestion - Serve with Castoro Chardonnay or Fume Blanc.

CHATEAU JULIEN WINERY

Chateau Julien Winery is nestled comfortably in the bucolic ambiance of Central California's Carmel Valley. Beginning in 1982, owners Robert and Patricia Brower cultivated and nurtured not only award-winning wines but a stellar reputation rivaled by few in the rich California wine industry. The French country chateau is located just 15 minutes from Monterey.

Since its grand opening in June 1984, the winery has won more than 390 awards in both national and international competitions. Chateau Julien produces Merlot, private reserve Chardonnay, Semillion, Sauvignon Blanc, Johannisberg Riesling and Gewurztraminer, along with limited quantities of award-winning Cabernets. The ultimate goal of the winery is being achieved by the staff's dedication towards production of the finest Chardonnay and Cabernet Sauvignon.

✗ *This colorful stir-fry from Bill Anderson, winemaker at Chateau Julien, is beautiful to look at, a snap to prepare, tasty and good for you. Serve with crusty French bread and wild rice.*

SUMMERTIME SCALLOP STIR-FRY
4 portions

4 tablespoons virgin olive oil
1/2 pound mushrooms, sliced
1/2 pound green beans, trimmed, cut into 1-inch pieces
1 head broccoli, stems discarded, flowers only
1 green bell pepper, cored, seeded and cut into strips
1 yellow bell pepper, cored, seeded and cut into strips
1 red bell pepper, cored, seeded and cut into strips
1 bunch green onions, trimmed and sliced
4 cloves garlic, finely minced
2 tablespoons finely chopped fresh tarragon
1/2 cup guava-passion fruit juice
1 pound fresh sea scallops
Salt and freshly ground black pepper, to taste

1 Heat 2 tablespoons of the olive oil over high heat in a very large skillet or wok. When it is hot, sauté the mushrooms until they give off their juices. Add all the other vegetables, except the garlic and tarragon. Stir-fry for 2 minutes. Add the garlic to the skillet. Cover and cook for 1 minute more.

2 Reduce the heat to a very low simmer and add the tarragon and guava-passion fruit juice. Keep warm.

3   In a small skillet add the remaining olive oil. When it is very hot add the scallops and sauté quickly, until they are barely cooked through. Watch carefully, so the scallops do not overcook.

4   Salt and pepper the scallops and add them to the vegetables. Serve immediately.

Wine Suggestion - Serve with Chateau Julien Gewurztraminer or Johannisberg Riesling.

CHOUINARD VINEYARDS

With its terraced vineyards, woodsy hillsides and restored red-barn winery, Chouinard Vineyards is one of the most picturesque spots in the Bay area. Set in the folds of the historic Palomares Canyon, the winery produces award-winning, hand-crafted varietals including a distinctive Granny Smith apple wine.

The owners, George, Caroline and Damian Chouinard's, philosophy is to specialize in the production of small lots of wine with an emphasis on unique style. They choose a broad range of varietals from their own vineyards, in addition to select vineyards in Monterey, Livermore, and the North Central Coast appellations.

With a production of 4,500 cases of Chardonnay, Chenin Blanc, Johannisberg Riesling, Cabernet Sauvignon, Gewurztraminer and Petite Syrah, Chouinard Vineyards is located in the rolling hills west of the Livermore Valley between the historic towns of Sunol and Niles.

✗ *This recipe is a very unusual, wholesome meal when a vegetarian dish is in order. It is simple to scale up or down and freezes well. Steamed rice and a simple tossed green salad complete this meal.*

DAMIAN CHOUINARD'S INDIAN CHILI
8 portions

3 tablespoons vegetable oil
2 onions, coarsely chopped
2 green bell peppers, cored, seeded and coarsely chopped
1 red bell pepper, cored, seeded and coarsely chopped
1 teaspoon ground coriander
1 teaspoon ground cumin
1 teaspoon tumeric
1/2 teaspoon cayenne pepper
1/2 teaspoon mustard seeds
1/2 teaspoon freshly ground black pepper
3 cloves garlic, finely minced
1 tablespoon fresh ginger, finely minced
2 cans (16 ounces each) stewed tomatoes
2 cans (16 ounces each) dark red kidney beans, with juice
1/2 pound raw, unsalted cashew nuts
1/8 pound pine nuts
2 cups raisins
2 cardamon pods, crushed (optional)

1 Heat the vegetable oil in a very large skillet or Dutch oven over medium heat. Add the onions, green and red bell peppers and sauté until just tender, 5 to 7 minutes.

2 Add the coriander, cumin, turmeric, cayenne pepper, mustard seeds, black pepper, garlic and ginger. Sauté briefly until the spices are aromatic.

3 Stir in the stewed tomatoes, kidney beans, cashews, pine nuts, raisins and cardamon, if using. Add some water if the chili seems dry. Reduce the heat to low and simmer for 30 to 40 minutes.

Wine Suggestion - Serve with Chouinard Gewurztraminer.

CLAIBORNE & CHURCHILL VINTNERS

Claiborne & Churchill is a small, premium winery located in the Edna Valley outside of San Luis Obispo. The winery was founded by Claiborne Thompson and Fredericka Churchill in 1983 to produce dry dinner wines similar in style to the wines made in the French province of Alsace. In keeping with traditional Alsatian winemaking techniques, they produce wines in which firm structure and rich texture are as important as varietal character and fruit. The resulting dry wines made from Riesling, Gewurztraminer and Muscat grapes are versatile food wines that enhance the more traditional flavors of European and American cooking, as well as the spicier, exotic flavors of California, Southwestern and Far Eastern cuisines.

Claiborne & Churchill also produces small lots of other wines such as Chardonnay and Pinot Noir. Grapes are purchased on a select basis from the cool, maritime valleys of the Central Coast. Production is limited to a few thousand cases per year.

✗ *Paella is the perfect party dish. The possibilities of ingredient combinations are endless.*

PAELLA PACIFICA
10 to 12 portions

1/2 cup flour
1 teaspoon salt
Freshly ground black pepper to taste
1 teaspoon paprika
12 chicken drummettes
6 tablespoons olive oil
2 medium onions, coarsely chopped
3 cloves garlic, minced
1 cup tomatoes, peeled, seeded and coarsely chopped
2 linguica sausages, sliced in 1/4 inch pieces
2 1/2 cups rice, preferably Basmati*
6 cups chicken broth, heated to boiling
1 teaspoon Spanish saffron
12 medium shrimp, peeled and deveined
1 cup bay scallops
12 clams, well scrubbed
12 mussels, well scrubbed and bearded**
1 cup Claiborne & Churchill Gewurztraminer
1 package (10 ounces) frozen peas, thoroughly defrosted
1/4 cup capers, drained
1 jar (4 ounces) pimientos, drained and sliced or 1
    roasted red pepper, peeled and sliced

* Basmati rice is a wonderfully flavored, aromatic rice. It is available at health food stores or gourmet markets. Rinse it well before using.

** Do not beard mussels until right before you are ready to cook them, or they will die and spoil.

1 Place the flour, salt, pepper and paprika in a large paper bag and mix thoroughly. Pat the chicken pieces dry with paper towels and add to the flour mixture a few at a time and shake until the chicken is well coated. Shake off excess flour and set aside. In a heavy, 12-inch skillet or paella pan, heat the olive oil until a light haze forms above it. Add the chicken and brown it well, turning the pieces with tongs and regulating the heat so they color evenly without burning. As the pieces become a rich golden brown, remove them to a plate and keep warm. In the same pan sauté the onion and garlic over medium heat until soft and golden, about 10 to 15 minutes. Add the tomatoes and cook briefly. Set tomato mixture aside.

2 Place the linguica slices in a saucepan and cover with cold water. Bring the water to a boil over high heat. Then reduce the heat to low and simmer, uncovered, for 5 minutes to remove excess color and spice. Drain water and add sausage to the paella pan.

3 Put the paella pan back on the burner over high heat. Stir in the rice and cook until it starts to turn translucent, stirring constantly. Reduce the heat to medium and add about half of the chicken broth and all of the saffron and cook, stirring gently, for five minutes. Stir in the shrimp and scallops and continue to simmer uncovered, until the rice absorbs most of the broth and is almost done. Add more broth as necessary.

4 In a separate saucepan, steam the clams and mussels in 1 cup of Gewurztraminer until the shells start to open. Remove from the wine and set aside, discarding any clams and mussels that have not opened.

5 Just before the rice mixture is done, stir in the peas, capers and chicken drummettes. Arrange the clams and mussels on top of the rice, and garnish with strips of pimiento. When the paella is done, remove it from the stove and drape a kitchen towel loosely over the top. Let it rest for 5 to 10 minutes. Place the paella pan in the center of the table for your guests to admire and help themselves.

Wine Suggestion - Serve with the remainder of the Claiborne & Churchill Gewurztraminer.

CORBETT CANYON VINEYARDS

Corbett Canyon Vineyards is located in the Edna Valley just south of San Luis Obispo.

The winery produces premium vintage-dated varietal wines. It specializes in Chardonnay produced from grapes grown on the estate vineyard known as Northwood, located in the Los Alamos Valley, found in northern Santa Barbara County. Corbett Canyon wines are an excellent companion to many foods.

Salmon with a creamy sauce always works well with Chardonnay. This is wonderful with grilled new potatoes and a bright vegetable.

GRILLED SALMON WITH SHIITAKE SAUCE

4 portions

1 cup (2 sticks) unsalted butter, at room temperature
1/2 pound shiitake mushrooms, sliced
3 tablespoons white wine vinegar
3 tablespoons Corbett Canyon Chardonnay
1 shallot, peeled and finely minced
Salt and freshly ground white pepper, to taste
1/2 cup fresh basil leaves, thinly sliced
4 salmon fillets (about 7 ounces each), skin on and pin-boned
Freshly squeezed juice of 1 lemon
1 lemon, sliced into 4 wedges, for garnish
Fresh basil for garnish

1 Prepare hot coals for grilling.

2 In a medium skillet melt 3 tablespoons of the butter over medium-high heat. Add the mushrooms and sauté until tender, about 5 minutes. Pour the butter from the mushrooms into a small bowl to use as a baste for the salmon. Set aside.

3 Combine the vinegar, wine and shallots in a saucepan. Cook rapidly over high heat until the liquid has almost all evaporated, 1 to 2 minutes. Remove from the heat.

4 Add the rest of the butter, 1 tablespoon at a time, whisking constantly, until the butter is incorporated and the sauce is creamy. Season to taste with salt and white pepper. Gently stir in the mushrooms and basil leaves. Keep warm.

5   Grill the salmon fillets, skin side up, over the hot coals for 1 to 2 minutes. Turn the fillets and pour some lemon juice over each one and baste with the shiitake butter. Continue cooking until the desired doneness is reached.

6   Remove the skin from the salmon and place the salmon on a serving platter. Garnish with lemon wedges and fresh basil leaves. Spoon the mushroom sauce over the salmon. Serve immediately.

Wine Suggestion - Delicious with Corbett Canyon Vineyards Chardonnay.

COTTONWOOD CANYON VINEYARD
AND WINERY

The picturesque Cottonwood Canyon Vineyard is so named because of the large and beautiful cottonwood trees standing in this beautiful setting. The vineyard consists of 46 acres of Chardonnay and 6 acres of Pinot Noir, which was recently planted in the canyon.

Norman and Sharon Beko chose their Santa Maria Valley locations primarily because of the climate. The vines receive the warmth of the morning and mid-day sun with the major influences of the ocean breezes in the late afternoon and evening. The always-present summer fog creates the perfect environment for the growth of premium-wine grapes. To further improve the grape quality, Cottonwood Canyon uses labor-intensive but beneficial techniques such as exposing the berries to even more sun by pulling leaves from around the clusters and hand-harvesting.

Plans are currently underway for the construction of a winery that will be built into the canyon hill in harmony with its environment. Storage caves and a tasting room will also be located in the beautiful canyon. It will be surrounded by herb gardens for the gourmet kitchen where the emphasis will be placed on the synthesis of wine and cuisine.

✄ *The pungent flavors of the Savoy cabbage and the lemon thyme enhance the flavor of the chicken breasts. The cream mellows it out, making it prefect for a special winter dinner with a bottle of Chardonnay.*

❧

CHICKEN BREASTS WITH SAVOY CABBAGE
AND CRIMINI MUSHROOMS
6 portions

For the sauce
4 cups low sodium chicken stock, preferably homemade
1 cup Cottonwood Canyon Chardonnay
1/2 cup mushroom stems
2 bay leaves
1 sprig fresh thyme
1 1/2 cups heavy cream

For the main dish
1 tablespoon olive oil
3 whole chicken breasts (6 halves), skinned, boned
*   and patted dry*
3 tablespoons butter
1/2 pound crimini mushrooms, cleaned, stems
*   removed for sauce*
1 cup carrots, peeled, quartered and cut into 3-inch lengths

1 cup parsnips, peeled, quartered and cut into 3-inch lengths
1/4 cup finely minced shallots
*1 small head Savoy cabbage, halved, cored and cut
    into 1-inch ribbons*
1/4 cup Cottonwood Canyon Chardonnay
1/4 cup chicken stock, preferably homemade
Salt and freshly ground black pepper, to taste
2 tablespoons finely chopped fresh lemon thyme
*2 tablespoons balsamic vinegar or freshly squeezed
    lemon juice*
1 teaspoon freshly ground nutmeg
4 tablespoons finely chopped fresh Italian parsley

To make the sauce

1   In a non-reactive saucepan, over medium heat, combine the chicken stock, wine, mushroom stems, bay leaves and fresh thyme. Boil this mixture until it is reduced to one third its original volume, about 1 1/2 cups. Remove from the heat.

2   Strain the sauce through a sieve, pressing hard on the solids to extract all the juices. Discard the mushroom stems. Set the sauce aside and keep it warm.

To prepare the chicken breasts, mushrooms and vegetables

1   Heat the olive oil in a large sauté pan over medium-high heat. Sauté the chicken breasts until they are golden brown on each side. Remove and keep warm.

2   Add 2 tablespoons of the butter to the same pan and sauté the mushrooms until they are lightly browned. Remove the mushrooms with a slotted spoon and keep warm.

3   Add the remaining butter to the sauté pan and add the carrots, parsnips and shallots. Sauté 1 to 2 minutes. Then add the cabbage and sauté until the cabbage starts to wilt, about 1 minute more.

4   Add the wine, chicken stock, salt, pepper, thyme and vinegar to the sauté pan and bring to a boil. Add the mushrooms and mix just enough to incorporate the ingredients. Lay the chicken breasts on top of the vegetables and cook for 8 to 10 minutes, uncovered, until most of the liquid has boiled away.

5   Meanwhile, bring the sauce back to a boil and add the cream. Cook over medium-high heat until it is thickened and the volume is reduced to 2 cups.

6   Arrange a bed of vegetables on each plate and place 1 chicken breast on top. Nap each breast with about 1/4 cup of the reserved sauce. Dust each breast with nutmeg and sprinkle with chopped parsley. Serve immediately.

Wine Suggestion - Delicious with Cottonwood Canyon Chardonnay.

CRESTON VINEYARDS

Located on 569 acres of gravelly limestone soil, high in the La Panza Mountains, Creston Vineyards can be found by driving east on Highway 58 from Highway 101. At Creston Vineyards they blend the best of French philosophy, tradition and finesse, with state-of-the-art California technology. Their handmade wines respect the grape, never masking the fine flavors of the fruit.

The grapes are harvested from estate and select vineyards by trained hands and appropriately fermented and aged in French oak barrels. The family winery is hands-on, whether in the vineyards, on the tractor, or handling the irrigation system, checking the bottling line or working in the tasting room. The personal effort at Creston Vineyard is a continuing labor of love. At Creston they believe in giving their varietals this much attention because they are wine lovers first and producers second.

✗ *Brown rice or orzo and a tossed salad with lots of fresh celery completes this healthy meal.*

SPA STYLE MEAT LOAF
4 portions

1 pound super lean ground beef or veal
1/4 pound fresh mushrooms, sliced
1 can (7 ounces) salsa, any kind
2 tablespoons dehydrated minced onions
1/4 cup barbecue sauce (optional)

1 Preheat the oven to 350°F.

2 Combine the ground beef, mushrooms, salsa and dehydrated onions in a mixing bowl, and mix thoroughly with your hands.

3 With damp hands form the mixture into an oval and place in a baking dish. Cook for 1 hour until done.

4 If you are using the barbecue sauce, spread it over the top after 30 minutes of baking to form a glaze.

Wine Suggestion - Serve with Creston Vineyards Pinot Noir, Merlot or Zinfandel.

EDNA VALLEY VINEYARD

Located north of Santa Barbara in San Luis Obispo County, the Edna Valley Vineyard is conspicuous for its production of superbly crafted yet affordable Chardonnay and Pinot Noir wines. Rich in varietal character, stylish and complex with a fine balance, they explode the old theory that premium California winemaking is the exclusive domain of the Napa and Sonoma Valleys.

The Edna Valley viticultural area is blessed with a relatively cool, mild climate, not unlike that of the Chablis and Burgundy wine regions of France. Thanks to its east-west orientation, the Edna Valley benefits from the marine winds that flow from nearby Morro Bay, in effect producing a highly desirable form of "natural air-conditioning." This and excellent soil conditions render the Edna Valley a wine-producing region of the first order, especially where Chardonnay and Pinot Noir are concerned.

The Edna Valley Vineyard, which bears the name of this splendid viticultural area, is the fruit of the successful alliance between Paragon Vineyard Company, owned by the Niven family, and the Chalone Wine Group of San Francisco. The Chalone Wine Group has made a name for itself as the only publicly held company in the United States whose primary concern is the production and marketing of premium wines.

✘*A delicious combination of classic flavors, this chicken is a natural with Chardonnay. Serve with wild rice and a colorful vegetable.*

CHICKEN WITH TARRAGON CREAM
6 portions

6 chicken legs or thighs
Salt and freshly ground black pepper, to taste
4 tablespoons unsalted butter
6 ounces Italian brown mushrooms, sliced
1/2 cup chopped red onion
1 tablespoon flour
1 can (14 ounces) low sodium chicken broth
1 cup heavy or whipping cream
3 tablespoons fresh tarragon sprigs, finely chopped
1 tablespoon fresh lemon juice

1 Sprinkle the chicken with salt and pepper. Melt the butter in a large skillet or Dutch oven over medium-high heat. Brown the chicken pieces on all sides, about 10 minutes. Remove the chicken and set aside.

2   Drain the excess fat from the skillet, leaving in 1 tablespoon to sauté the vegetables. Add the mushrooms and onions to the skillet and sauté them for 4 minutes, until the mushrooms have given off their juices and the onions are softened.

3   Add the flour and cook 1 minute, stirring constantly. Add the chicken broth, heavy cream and tarragon and bring to a boil. Cook for 5 minutes.

4   Return the chicken to the pan. Cover and simmer until the chicken is tender, about 20 minutes.

5   Remove the chicken to a warmed serving platter. Cook the sauce until it is reduced and slightly thickened. Add the lemon juice and adjust seasonings, if needed. Pour the sauce over the chicken and serve immediately.

Wine Suggestion - Serve with Edna Valley Chardonnay.

EMERALD BAY WINERY

Emerald Bay Winery is one of the Chateau Julien Winery labels. It is nestled comfortably in the bucolic ambiance of Central California's Carmel Valley. Beginning in 1982, owners Robert and Patricia Brower cultivated and nurtured award-winning wines but, a stellar reputation rivaled by few in the rich California wine traditions. The French country chateau is located just 15 minutes from Monterey.

Since its grand opening in June 1984, the winery has won more than 390 awards in both national and international competitions. The winery produces Merlot, private reserve Chardonnay, Semillion, Sauvignon Blanc, Johannisberg Riesling and Gewurztraminer, along with limited quantities of award-winning Cabernets.

✗ *This is a tasty and simple preparation for pork. Serve with fresh green beans and new potatoes.*

PORK LOIN IN CHARDONNAY
6 portions

3 to 4 cloves garlic, finely minced
1 tablespoon fresh lemon juice
1/4 cup olive oil
1/4 cup low sodium soy sauce or tamari
1/4 cup Emerald Bay Chardonnay
3 pounds boneless pork loin roast
1/4 cup Dijon mustard
1 sprig fresh rosemary, leaves only

1 Preheat the oven to 350ºF.

2 In a small bowl add the garlic, lemon juice, olive oil, soy sauce and Chardonnay. Stir until well combined. Pour this marinade over the pork tenderloin in a shallow baking dish. Rub the mustard into the pork and sprinkle the rosemary on top. Marinate for 1 hour.

3 Roast the pork for 45 minutes or until an instant reading meat thermometer registers 150ºF. at the thickest part. Remove the pan from the oven and let it rest 10 minutes.

4 Slice the pork into 1/2 inch slices and serve.

Wine Suggestion - Serve with Emerald Bay Chardonnay.

FIRESTONE VINEYARD

Firestone Vineyard lays claim for having been the first winery in the Santa Ynez Valley and is located amid a quiet pastoral area of rolling hills punctuated by gnarled oaks. It is a majestic winery overlooking 260 acres of vineyards. Firestone offers daily tours through cathedral-like cellars of row upon row of oak barrels and casks.

Since the first harvest in 1975, the wines at Firestone have steadily gained in reputation. Award-winning Riesling, Gewurztraminer, Merlot, Chardonnay, Cabernet Sauvignon and Sauvignon Blanc are distributed throughout the world.

The special mission of Brooks Firestone has always been to make excellent wines at affordable prices. Winemaker Alison Green, renowned for her precise palate and technical skill, employs traditional practices supplemented with new techniques when they are found to enhance and accelerate the pursuit of excellence.

✗*Patrick Will is the general manager at Firestone Vineyard and a "Grand Wizard of California wine." The figs in the sauce add an unctuous quality that should not be missed during the fig season. Serve with a bright orange squash and broccoli.*

⚘

PATRICK WILL'S TENDERLOIN OF PORK WITH FIG BEURRE ROUGE
4 portions

> 2 pounds pork tenderloin
> Olive oil
> Salt, to taste
> 1 teaspoon freshly ground black pepper
> 1/2 cup balsamic vinegar
> 1 teaspoon whole black peppercorns
> 3 tablespoons finely minced shallots
> 1 cup Firestone Vineyard Merlot
> 1 sprig fresh rosemary
> 8 tablespoons (1 stick) unsalted butter, room temperature
> 1 cup fresh figs, unpeeled and chopped
> 8 fig halves for garnish

1 Preheat oven to 350°F. Place the pork tenderloin in a shallow roasting pan, and rub it all over with olive oil, sprinkle it with salt, and cover with the ground pepper. Cover with foil. Cook for 30 minutes, until a meat thermometer reads 140°F. or until meat is slightly pink in the center. Let the meat rest for 15 minutes before slicing.

2   In a small sauce pan combine the vinegar, peppercorns, shallots, wine and rosemary. Cook the mixture over high heat until the volume is reduced by one half. Strain the mixture and discard the solids.

3   Put the sauce back in the saucepan, reduce heat to low, and add the figs. When the figs are warm, add the butter 1 tablespoon at a time, stirring constantly until the sauce is thick and glossy. Add salt to taste.

4   Cut the pork into 1/2 inch-thick slices and serve topped with a small amount of sauce. Garnish with fresh fig halves.

Wine Suggestion - Serve with Firestone Merlot.

THE GAINEY VINEYARD

The Gainey Vineyard is part of the 1800-acre Gainey Ranch located in the beautiful Santa Ynez Valley. Recognized as the heart of Santa Barbara's wine country, the valley is blessed with cool ocean breezes and moderate temperatures that make this one of the nation's leading viticultural areas.

In 1984, after two years of research and development, Daniel J. Gainey opened the 12,000-square-foot winery and visitor facility on the northern boundary of the Gainey Ranch. Son, Daniel H. Gainey, joined forces with his dad in 1986 to make the Gainey Vineyard one of the most vital and well-respected premium wineries in Santa Barbara County.

As winemaker for the Gainey Vineyard, Rick Longoria consistently crafts well-balanced, award-winning wines. His talents are showcased in his "limited selection" wine collection, which has garnered rave reviews from wine critics and consumers alike. Surrounded by 65 acres of estate-grown grapes, the Gainey Vineyard produces 12,000 to 15,000 cases of premium wine per year.

✗The meaty veal shanks are simmered in a light tomato sauce and traditionally served with risotto Milanese. Other options include couscous or pasta. The flavor improves with time, so make this one ahead.

OSSO BUCCO SANTA YNEZ
8 portions

4 tablespoons unsalted butter
2 onions, coarsely chopped
2 large carrots, coarsely chopped
2 stalks celery, chopped
6 to 8 cloves garlic, finely minced
8 sections of veal shank, 1 1/2 inches thick
Salt and freshly ground pepper, to taste
1/2 cup unbleached all-purpose flour
1/4 cup olive oil
2 cups Gainey Sauvignon Blanc
1 cup chicken stock, preferably homemade
1 teaspoon dried basil
1 teaspoon dried thyme
1/2 cup chopped fresh Italian parsley
2 bay leaves
1 can (28 ounces) Italian plum tomatoes, drained
  and coarsely chopped
1 tablespoon freshly grated orange zest

1   In a heavy, shallow casserole or Dutch oven melt the butter over medium heat. When the foam subsides, add the onions, carrots, celery and garlic. Sauté until the vegetables are lightly colored. Set aside.

2   Season each piece of veal on both sides generously with the salt and pepper. Dredge them in the flour, shaking off any excess.

3   In another large skillet, heat one half of the olive oil. Brown the veal shanks a few at a time over medium-high heat until they are well browned, adding oil as needed. Transfer veal to the Dutch oven with the vegetables, placing them side by side.

4   Preheat the oven to 350°F.

5   Discard the fat from the veal skillet and add the wine, scraping up any brown bits clinging to the pan. Reduce the wine by one half. Stir in the chicken stock, basil, thyme, parsley, bay leaves, tomatoes and orange zest. Bring this mixture to a boil and pour over the veal. Cover and bake for 1 1/2 hours or until tender.

6   Arrange the veal shanks on a heated platter and spoon the vegetables around them and serve.

Wine Suggestion - Osso Bucco is best accompanied by a bottle of Gainey Vineyard Merlot.

Georis Winery

Georis Winery is located in upper Carmel Valley, a valley that boasts the ideal soil conditions and microclimate to produce distinctive world-class red wines. In 1981 the predominantly Merlot vineyard was planted. Other varietal such as Cabernet Sauvignon, Cabernet Franc, Malbec and Petit Verdot were also planted as part of the blend known as Georis Merlot.

Walter Georis immigrated to the United States in 1956 from Malmedy, a small town in Belgium. From this heritage comes the symbols used on the wine label — the dragon of his home town framed by the sun. The text is in Walloon, an old romance language, and means "when the sun shines, it's for everyone." This is a saying common to the Ardennes.

The 1985 Merlot was the winery's first commercial release, and only 250 cases were produced. In order to maintain its high standards, current production is limited to approximately one thousand cases of estate-produced Merlot.

✗ *Serve the rabbit with steamed baby carrots and wild rice tossed with peas.*

Carmel Valley Rabbit
4 portions

1 whole rabbit, cut into serving pieces
1 1/2 bottles Georis Merlot
2 large onions, peeled and cut in half
2 heads garlic, separated into cloves, papery outside
  skin discarded
15 fresh sage leaves, or 1 teaspoon dried
1 small branch fresh rosemary
3 large wild mushrooms (shiitake, oyster, porcini, or
  chantrelles)
5 whole bay leaves
2 tablespoons honey
1 teaspoon salt, or to taste
Freshly ground black pepper, to taste

I   Combine all the ingredients in a large stock pot, and bring to a slow simmer. Cook, covered for 1 hour. Remove the rabbit pieces with a slotted spoon to a plate, and set aside.

2   Pour the Merlot sauce through a sieve, pressing hard on the solids to extract all the juices. Discard the solids. Put the rabbit back into the stock pot with the strained sauce. Cook, uncovered, over medium-low heat for 1 hour until the rabbit is tender and the wine is reduced to a thick glaze. Taste and correct seasonings.

Variation: Chicken may be substituted for the rabbit.

Wine Suggestion - Accompany with Georis Merlot.

HECKER PASS WINERY

Located in the Southern Santa Clara Valley at the foot of the Mount Madonna range is the Hecker Pass Winery. It was established in 1972 by a third-generation wine-making family, Mario and Frances Fortino.

The grapes for the premium, varietal table wines are grown at the winery, and their juice is naturally fermented and aged in redwood tanks and small oak casks. The wine is then bottle aged before being released. Individual wines, which include Petite Syrah, Zinfandel, Carignane and Grenache, may vary slightly from dry and light, to robust and hearty. Since 1974 the Hecker Pass Winery has won more than seventy awards.

Visitors will enjoy the rustic atmosphere of the tasting room, with its 20-foot long redwood bar that overlooks the vineyard and picnic area.

✘ *Oven-roasted potatoes and a salad of sliced tomatoes and mozzarella cheese with basil, olive oil, and red wine vinegar is a great way to complete this meal.*

GARLIC-CRUSTED LEG OF LAMB
8 portions

1 leg of lamb (5 to 6 pounds)
2 slices bacon
1/4 cup minced fresh Italian parsley
2 tablespoons unsalted butter, softened
1 tablespoon balsamic or sherry vinegar
4 cloves garlic, finely minced
1 teaspoon each: salt, paprika and freshly ground
*   black pepper*

1 Trim all visible fat from the surface of the lamb. Lightly score the top of the lamb in a diamond pattern cutting down about 1/4 inch. Pat the lamb dry with paper towels and set aside.

2 Combine all the other ingredients in the bowl of a food processor fitted with a steel blade. Pulse on and off until the ingredients are finely minced and form a paste. Do not over-mix.

3 Pat the garlic and herb mixture all over the lamb to form a crust. Place the lamb in a shallow roasting pan and refrigerate for 1 hour to help the crust to adhere to the lamb.

4   Preheat the oven to 325°F.

5   Place the pan on the center rack in the oven and roast for 2 1/2 hours, until the lamb is cooked to medium. Let the lamb rest, loosely covered, 15 minutes before carving.

Wine Suggestion - An excellent wine choice is the Hecker Pass Winery Petite Syrah Select or Zinfandel.

JUSTIN VINEYARDS AND WINERY

Both Justin and Deborah Baldwin, proprietors of Justin Vineyards and Winery, appreciate wine and the effort necessary to produce fine vintages. Together they have made the sacrifices necessary to assure a quality product, but they also have fun and enjoy the process. In 1981 Justin purchased 160 acres in the remote Adelaida Valley west of Paso Robles in California's Central Coast. The land was originally homesteaded by Mennonite church members in the 1860s and was used to dry farm barley for cattle feeding.

The year 1987 saw the first crush at the winery. This was the beginning of the winery's policy of 100 percent estate production of Justin wines. The wine is and always will be 100 percent estate grown, produced and bottled and the winery will remain a family business. The goal at Justin Vineyards and Winery is to bring only the highest quality wine to the market.

The Justin products represent a good value for their market category and present the consumer with a unique, superior and affordable product. The philosophy at Justin is to have fun along the way, make good wine, make a fair profit, and celebrate the social and fraternal contributions wine has made to our culture.

✗ *This is actually a warm scallop salad dressed up for a special occasion. It is low in fat as well as delicious and colorful.*

GRILLED SCALLOPS AND SHIITAKE MUSHROOMS WITH LEEK "CONFIT"
4 portions

16 medium (8 ounces) shiitake mushrooms
4 leeks, well rinsed and patted dry
Olive oil
1 small bunch fresh chives, finely minced
Freshly squeezed juice of 1 lime
1 tablespoon Dijon mustard
1 tablespoon finely minced fresh tarragon
1 tablespoon unsalted butter
*3/4 pound sea scallops, tough connective tissue
    removed, rinsed and patted dry*
Salt and freshly ground black pepper, to taste

1   Preheat the oven to 375°F. Remove the stems from the shiitake mushrooms and place the mushrooms on an ungreased baking sheet. Set aside.

2   Trim the leeks by cutting off the dark green tops and the root end. Save the tops. Cut the leeks in half, vertically, then cut into 1-inch lengths. Add the light part of the leeks to the mushrooms and place in the preheated oven for 20 to 30 minutes, until the natural sugars begin to caramelize. Remove from the oven and set aside.

3   Chop the dark green leek tops into small pieces. In a medium skillet over low heat sauté the leek greens in 3 tablespoons olive oil, with the chives for about 10 minutes, until the greens are softened. Remove from the heat.

4   Place the greens in a blender and puree until smooth. Transfer the puree to a glass 2-cup measure and add olive oil to measure 2/3 cup. Stir in the lime juice, mustard, tarragon, and salt and pepper, if desired. Correct seasonings and set aside.

5   In a large skillet melt the butter over high heat. Add the scallops and sauté quickly until just barely tender, about 3 minutes. Season with salt and freshly ground black pepper.

6   To serve, transfer the roasted shiitake mushrooms to four plates, dividing them evenly. Toss the roasted leeks with some of the leek vinaigrette, just to moisten. Mound the leek "confit" in the center of each plate. Place the scallops on top of the shiitake mushrooms and drizzle with the remaining vinaigrette. Serve immediately.

Wine Suggestion - Serve with the Justin Vineyards and Winery Chardonnay.

LANE TANNER WINERY

In 1984 Lane Tanner started her own company with one client. She agreed to make wine for the Hitching Post restaurant (a locally famous Santa Barbara County steak house). She started out making Chardonnay and Pinot Noir, and her methods for Pinot Noir production have changed very little over the past seven years. She uses the best grapes available in Santa Barbara County and is the only winemaker that has bottled a Sierra Madre Vineyard Pinot Noir from 1985 to the present.

Tanner harvests the grapes when they taste right, not when the sugar hits a certain number. In the first picking she looks for character and structure. In the second picking she looks for complexity and fruit maturity.

Currently, Pinot Noir is the only wine she produces. Tanner believes that Pinot Noir is the most responsive, delicate, fickle and fragile grape and is completely hooked on it. Production at Lane Tanner is limited because she cannot stand anyone else touching her "babies." Lane Tanner is a product for people who are searching for the more subtle elegant nuances of the Pinot Noir grape.

Lane is known for her unique cooking style. Her unlikely combination of ingredients is always unusual and inspiring. Serve this very tasty curry over steamed rice.

LANE'S ORIGINAL CHICKEN CURRY
6 portions

12 chicken thighs, rinsed and patted dry
2 large onions, peeled and diced
7 large garlic cloves, finely minced
2 cans double-strength chicken stock
4 cups water
1 cup Lane Tanner Pinot Noir
4 tablespoons curry powder, regular and hot
2 teaspoons salt
2 tablespoons Worcestershire sauce
1/4 cup coconut or rice wine vinegar
1/2 cup Italian parsley, finely minced
1 small head green cabbage, chopped
1 teaspoon Garam Masala
1 can (14 ounces) coconut milk
Cooked rice

1 In a large stock pot add the chicken thighs, onions, garlic, stock, water, Pinot Noir and 2 tablespoons of the curry powder. Bring the mixture to a rolling boil over high heat. Reduce the heat to medium and cook, uncovered, for 1 1/2 hours.

2 With a slotted spoon remove the chicken from the pot and let it cool slightly. When it is cool enough to handle, remove the skin and bones. Cover the chicken and refrigerate while finishing the dish.

3 Skim the fat from the surface of the broth. Add the rest of the curry powder, salt, Worcestershire sauce, coconut vinegar, parsley and cabbage and continue to cook over medium heat for 30 minutes. The cabbage should be completely cooked, and the broth slightly thickened.

4 Add the Garam Masala, coconut milk and reserved chicken to the pot. Cook just long enough to warm the ingredients. Taste and correct seasonings. Serve over rice.

Wine Suggestion - With the curry drink a full-bodied Pinot Noir, such as the Lane Tanner Sanford and Benedict Vineyard Pinot Noir.

Leeward Winery

Leeward Winery was founded in 1979 by Chuck Brigham and Chuck Gardner at the Channel Islands Harbor. A view of the harbor is featured on their label. Leeward has become nationally renowned for the quality of the fine wines produced.

The winery is particularly well known for the excellence of its Chardonnays and is recognized as one of the premier producers of this variety from the Central Coast. The hand-crafted style of the wines is self-evident, and the use of nothing but French oak cooperage is typical of Leeward's commitment to producing the highest possible quality of wines. Other varietals produced by Leeward include Pinot Noir, Cabernet Sauvignon and Merlot.

✖ *Serve with steamed or sautéed carrots and a salad.*

❧

Leeward Chicken In Puff Pastry
4 portions

7 ounces Feta cheese, preferably French sheep's milk Feta
8 tablespoons olive oil
3 tablespoons finely chopped fresh dill
1 pound fresh spinach, well rinsed and trimmed
4 boneless, skinless chicken breasts
1 package (1 pound) frozen puff pastry, thawed
1 egg white

1   In a small bowl mix the Feta cheese, 4 tablespoons of the olive oil and the dill. Set aside.

2   In a large skillet add the spinach and cook it over low heat until it is wilted, using the water that clings to its leaves, about 4 to 5 minutes. Drain the spinach, squeezing out as much moisture as possible. Chop it coarsely and set aside to cool.

3   Rinse the chicken pieces well and trim away any excess fat. Pat them dry with paper towels. Place the breasts on a cutting surface skin side down. Remove the fillets (the finger-size muscle on the back of each breast half) and reserve them for another use. Place a piece of waxed paper or plastic wrap over each breast and pound it with the flat side of a meat pounder until thin.

4   In a large heavy skillet add the remaining olive oil and heat until the oil ripples on the top surface. Add the chicken pieces and quickly sauté until golden brown on each side. Do not cook the breasts completely, as they will finish cooking in the oven. Let the chicken cool for 30 minutes.

5   Lightly flour a work surface and roll the puff pastry out to a thickness of 1/4 inch. Cut into 4 equal pieces.

6   Lay 1 chicken breast on each puff pastry sheet. Spread the Feta cheese mixture over each breast, about 1/4 inch thick. Divide the cooked spinach evenly between the 4 chicken breasts and place it in the middle of each one. Roll up the chicken and pastry to form a tube. Using some water, wet the seams and ends of the puff pastry and seal.

7   Prick the top of the pastry 3 times with a fork and brush with the egg white. Place the pastries seam side down on a baking sheet and bake at 375°F. for 30 minutes, until golden brown. Serve whole or cut each pastry in thirds to expose the colorful filling.

Wine Suggestion - Leeward's Edna Valley Chardonnay, with its ripe tropical fruit aromas will complement the herbal spice and rich texture of this entree.

THE OJAI VINEYARD

In the spring of 1981, the Ojai Vineyard was planted to Syrah, Sauvignon Blanc and Semillion grapes. It was the first planting of commercial quantities (if that is what you can call 5.5 acres) of grapes in the Ojai Valley since the days of prohibition. Because of its proximity to the ocean, it is the ideal location for the varieties the winemaker planted.

In 1984 a tiny, well insulated and temperature-controlled winery was built and the Ojai Vineyard began making wines from its own grapes. Because of Adam and Helen Tolmach's fondness for traditionally crafted European wines, ancient, low-technology practices were adopted. While they are not afraid to utilize modern techniques to monitor the progress of the wine, natural, non-interventionist methods are preferred.

Now producing about three thousand cases a year, they find it is a very comfortable amount of wine to produce. They are able to run the harvest themselves, and do not need to delegate any part of the winemaking process to anyone else. They feel that this is where the fun is, and this is what makes the creative juices flow. Sales and administration is okay, but at the Ojai Vineyard, they believe that paying attention to every detail in the winemaking process and making the finest wines possible is far more satisfying.

✂ *Adam Tolmach says "I have never been known as one who follows recipes, but for this batch of barbecue sauce, I found a 1/4 cup measure and came up with these quantities. This is enough sauce for two large or three small chickens."*

CHICKEN BARBECUE
8 portions

1 29-ounce can tomato sauce
1/4 cup soy sauce or tamari
1/4 cup freshly ground cumin
1/4 cup freshly ground coriander
1/2 cup medium hot chili powder
1/4 cup very hot chili powder
3/4 cup balsamic vinegar
1 cup firmly packed brown sugar
1/4 cup Dijon mustard
5 large cloves garlic, finely minced
2 large or 3 small chickens, cut into serving pieces

1   Combine all the ingredients, except the chickens, in a medium saucepan and simmer, uncovered, for 20 to 30 minutes or until the sauce is reduced and fairly thick. Remove from heat and cool to room temperature.

2 Prepare an oak or charcoal fire in a Weber kettle. Place the chicken pieces on the grill and cover with the lid. Cook the chicken slowly, turning them occasionally until the chicken pieces are almost done, about 25 minutes.

3 Baste the chicken pieces generously with the sauce, and keep turning them until they are cooked through and slightly charred.

4 When the chicken is done, place it in a large bowl and liberally baste with the remaining sauce.

Wine Suggestion - Serve with The Ojai Vineyard Syrah.

PARAISO SPRINGS VINEYARDS

Paraiso Springs Vineyards is located on Paraiso Springs Road off the Arroyo Seco exit from U.S. Highway 101 south of Soledad. It is a 400-acre ranch in the Santa Lucia Highlands, 250 acres of which are planted to varietal winegrapes.

There are small canyons of Pinot Blanc and Chardonnay tucked along the rolling hills, and Gewurztraminer, Johannisberg Riesling and Pinot Noir grow on the leeward slopes of the Santa Lucia mountain range, which parts the Salinas Valley from the Pacific Coast.

The Smith family has chosen the very best fruit from their vineyards for their wines. Style and taste are evolving as Rich and Claudia make wines that they enjoy — wines that complement food and reflect the character of the cool Santa Lucia Highlands.

✗This exquisite duck is from Melac's Restaurant in Pacific Grove. It is simply excellent. Serve with wild rice pilaf.

❧

PARAISO SPRINGS DUCK WITH PINOT NOIR SAUCE
4 to 8 portions

1 bottle Paraiso Springs Pinot Noir
1/2 ounce dried cepe (porcini) mushrooms
4 sprigs fresh thyme
2 cloves garlic
8 cups duck or rich chicken stock, preferably homemade
8 boneless duck breasts, well rinsed and patted dry
Salt and freshly ground black pepper, to taste

1 In a heavy, non-reactive saucepan add the wine, mushrooms, thyme and garlic. Over high heat reduce the wine mixture to 1 cup. Add the duck stock and reduce by half its volume.

2 Remove the sauce from the heat and strain it through a fine sieve, pressing hard on the mushrooms to extract all their liquid. Return the sauce to the stove and reduce by one half again. Skim any foam from the surface of the sauce, remove it from the heat and keep warm.

3 Using a sharp knife, score the duck breasts through the skin in a crisscross pattern. Be sure to make a shallow incision, and be careful not to pierce the meat. Season both sides with salt and freshly ground black pepper.

4   In two sauté pans place the duck breasts skin side down and cook over medium-high heat until golden brown and the fat has been rendered, about 7 minutes. Turn the duck breasts and sear the meat for 30 to 90 seconds more. Remove the duck breasts from the pan and keep warm.

5   Slice the duck breasts into 1/4-inch slices and arrange them in a fan pattern on warm plates. Add any accumulated duck juices to the sauce and spoon the sauce over the duck. Serve immediately with a wild rice pilaf.

Wine Suggestion - The perfect accompaniment is Paraiso Springs Vineyards Pinot Noir.

PAUL MASSON VINEYARDS

From the time he first planted his vineyard, Paul Masson was guided by two basic convictions: fine varietals transplanted from the old world would create fine premium wines in the new world. Age-old European traditions of winemaking should be applied and adapted to achieve this goal.

Paul Masson sought and developed new areas for plantings and technologies to assist him in his work. He never lost sight of the fact that fine wine can only be produced by long years of knowledge, patience, care and pride. After all, Paul Masson sells no wine before its time.

This classic European-style dish is savory and well flavored. The flaming of the brandy makes this ideal for entertaining — remember to turn off the lights. Oven-roasted new potatoes and a salad round out the meal.

GAME HENS PAUL MASSON

6 portions

3 Cornish Game hens (about 1 1/2 pounds each), halved and backbones removed
2 cups Paul Masson Burgundy
1 teaspoon dried rosemary
2 cloves garlic, finely minced
The juice and grated rind of one lemon
5 tablespoons unsalted butter
1/2 cup chicken stock, preferably homemade
1 cucumber, peeled, seeded and cut into 1/2-inch thick discs
Salt and freshly ground pepper to taste
1/2 pound baby carrots, trimmed and boiled for 3 minutes
1/4 cup Paul Masson Brandy

1 Rinse the hen pieces well and pat dry. Discard the giblets or save them for another use.

2 Combine 1 cup of the Paul Masson Burgundy, rosemary, garlic, lemon juice and rind in a mixing bowl. Add the game hen halves and toss to coat well. Refrigerate for at least 30 minutes or up to 24 hours.

3 When you are ready to prepare the hens remove them from the marinade and pat them dry. Reserve the marinade for the sauce.

4   Melt 1 tablespoon of the butter in a large skillet over medium high heat. Add 3 Game hen halves and sauté for 5 minutes, turning once, until they are a nice golden brown. Remove the hens to a plate and add 1 more tablespoon of butter and the remaining hens to the skillet. Repeat the cooking process. Pour off any fat and return all the hen halves to the skillet.

5   Add the remaining 1 cup of Burgundy and the chicken stock to the skillet. Reduce the heat to low, cover and cook for 40 minutes or until done.

6   Remove the hens to a serving platter and keep warm.

7   Pour the marinade and pan juices into a medium saucepan and cook over high heat until the juices are reduced by one third their volume. Add the remaining 3 tablespoons butter, remove the saucepan from the heat and stir until the butter is incorporated and the sauce is glossy. Add the cucumber slices and keep warm.

8   Pour any accumulated juices from the hens back into the sauce and stir. Add salt and pepper to taste. Garnish the platter with the carrots and keep warm.

9   Meanwhile, warm the Brandy in a small pan, or in the microwave for 30 seconds and pour over the hens and flambé. When the flames die out, pour the wine sauce over the top of the hens and serve.

Wine Suggestion - Paul Masson Burgundy is the perfect wine for this dish.

PIEDRA CREEK WINERY

Piedra Creek Winery, probably the smallest bonded winery in the state, was founded in 1984. It is located on a knoll in the middle of the renowned MacGregor Chardonnay Vineyards in Edna Valley.

Typical total production is approximately 300 cases per year. The Chardonnay is essentially hand made and all production steps are personally performed by the winemaker, R.A. (Meo) Zuech. Half of the wine is fermented and aged in new French oak and the other half in one-year-old wood.

Most years Piedra Creek Chardonnay is rich and bold, to be equally enjoyed with your finest meals or on the back porch with your best friends.

✂ *A mixed green salad completes this entrée.*

❧

GAME HENS CHARDONNAY
3 to 6 portions

3 Cornish Game hens
Poultry seasoning, salt, freshly ground black pepper,
  garlic powder
5 tablespoons unsalted butter
15 sage leaves
3 small sprigs rosemary
3 tablespoons extra virgin olive oil
1/2 cup Piedra Creek Chardonnay
1/3 cup each finely chopped shallots, celery, parsley, carrots
1 clove garlic, finely minced
1 cup finely chopped mushrooms
2 tablespoons finely minced parsley
6 thick slices country sourdough bread

1 Remove giblets from Game hens and save for another use. Wash hens with cold water and pat dry with paper towels. Sprinkle cavities of hens with the poultry seasoning, salt, pepper and garlic powder. Stuff each with 1 tablespoon butter, 5 sage leaves, and 1 rosemary sprig. Truss each hen with string.

2 Heat the oil in a large skillet. Add the hens and brown on all sides. When hens are brown add the Chardonnay 1 tablespoon at a time for 2 to 3 minutes, then add the shallots, celery, 1/3 cup parsley, carrots and 1 more tablespoon butter. Cook over medium heat for about 5 minutes, stirring vegetables from time to time.

3   Preheat the oven to 350°F. Bake the Game hens, covered, for 30 minutes, then increase heat to 375°F. and bake 10 minutes longer. Remove from the oven and keep warm.

4   Meanwhile, melt the remaining 1 tablespoon butter in a skillet and lightly sauté the garlic, mushrooms and parsley until cooked through, about 3 to 4 minutes. Set aside.

5   Remove string from hens and cut each hen in half, saving all the juices. Toast the sourdough bread and place half a hen on each slice. Keep in a warm place until ready to serve.

6   Pour all the cooking juices through a strainer, pressing down on the solids to extract the liquid, discard solids. Skim and discard the accumulated fat from the top of the juices. Add the juices to the mushrooms. Salt to taste. Spoon the mushroom sauce over the hens and serve immediately.

Wine Suggestion - A Piedra Creek Winery Chardonnay is the perfect complement to this meal.

SAUCELITO CANYON VINEYARDS

After 20 years of working with the land and ten years of making wine commercially, Saucelito Canyon owner Bill Greenough knows his vineyard and winery well. It is the simplicity and the remoteness of the small winery, to the lack of electricity and high-tech equipment, that he and his wife Nancy appreciate. Working the land, picking the fruit and making the wine are all labors of love.

Although Saucelito Canyon shares a modern tasting room with Talley Vineyards in an historic adobe near Lopez Lake, one continues to appreciate the hidden, anachronistic gem that is Saucelito Canyon Vineyard. Enjoying the hard work and dedication — along with the sun, soil, vine, wood and time — creates a complete experience.

Bonded in 1982, Saucelito Canyon Vineyard Winery produces 1000 cases of estate-grown Zinfandel and 500 cases of estate-grown Cabernet Sauvignon annually. In addition to his award-winning wines, Greenough sells fruit to selected wineries for limited bottling.

This informative piece comes from Nancy Greenough: The term "venison" comes from the Latin term venatus, *which means "to hunt." The latter is probably akin to the Sanskrit term* venati, *which means "he desires, attacks or gains." Originally, the word venison applied to the flesh of any beast or bird of the chase but has now come to apply only to the flesh of deer. Venison has always been plentiful in the remote canyons and hills of upper Arroyo Grande Valley.*

Over the years we have had many opportunities for trying all sorts of marinades and cooking styles. Only just recently have I found one that has replaced all others. I love it for the simplicity and mellow complexity it adds to, not detracts from, the flavors of the game. Deer meat that has been properly dressed, skinned, trimmed and chilled should be treated like a prime cut of beef. Because venison fat is strong tasting, it must be trimmed away, and therefore, the roast could be cooked with added lard, salt pork or bacon. However, I like the fact that venison is not nearly as fatty as meat from a well-fed beef.

A lean venison roast before cooking contains, on the average, 75% water, 20% protein and 2% fat; a lean beef rump, 65 to 70% water, 20 to 23% protein, and 5 to 14% fat; and a lean leg of lamb, 67% water, 19% protein and 13% fat. Consequently, I do not lard the meat. I simply marinate the roast, or other cut, in buttermilk for 48 hours, refrigerated, turning night and morning — nothing else although I have seen suggestions for the addition of garlic and bay leaves.

Wild rice with mushrooms, freshly steamed spinach with a pat of butter round off the dish.

❦

Venison Saucelito

3 portions per pound of boneless roast

1 venison roast, any cut
1 cup buttermilk
2 tablespoons extra virgin olive oil
Wondra flour
Salt, freshly ground black pepper and paprika, to taste

1 Marinate the venison in the buttermilk for 48 hours.

2 Rinse the venison well and pat dry with paper towels. Rub it all over with the olive oil. Set it in a roasting pan.

3 Sprinkle the top with the Wondra flour, and then the salt, pepper and paprika.

4 Place the roast in a preheated 350°F. oven for 35 to 40 minutes per pound with the bone, or 20 to 25 minutes per pound without the bone, for medium-rare to medium. Remove from the oven and let it rest for 15 minutes before carving.

Wine Suggestion - Serve with Saucelito Zinfandel.

SILVER CANYON ESTATE WINES

"Somewhere north of Los Angeles, south of San Francisco, and east of Eden is a once and future land — the Middle Kingdom." The Silver Canyon Vineyards are the personification of this magical place, discovered by Marian Conway and her husband, Gary, more than twenty-five years ago.

The vineyards lie on the western-most tip of the Central Coast. At an elevation of 1300 feet, the sweeping hillsides are cradled by the Santa Lucia mountains just east of Hearst Castle. Known as the Adelaida region, the limestone soils and textbook microclimates are the envy of the wine world, producing wines so distinctive that they are redefining the California style of Chardonnay and Cabernet Sauvignon.

✗ *Serve this lovely entree with pasta or rice and asparagus or other seasonal green vegetable.*

CHARDONNAY POACHED SALMON WITH BASIL SAUCE
4 portions

1 tablespoon olive oil
3 tablespoons minced shallots
1/2 cup Silver Canyon Chardonnay
1/4 cup chicken stock, preferably homemade
1 tablespoon lemon juice
4 salmon fillets (6 ounces) skinned and boned
1/2 cup heavy or whipping cream
1/4 cup chopped fresh basil
Freshly ground white pepper, to taste
2 tablespoons unsalted butter, room temperature

1 Heat the olive oil in a large skillet over medium heat. Add the shallots and sauté until tender, about 2 minutes. Add the Chardonnay, chicken stock and lemon juice and bring to a simmer.

2 Add the salmon fillets to the skillet, cover and simmer 10 minutes, being careful not to boil.

3 Using a spatula, carefully transfer the fish to a tray and keep warm.

4 Cook the remaining liquid in the skillet until reduced to 1/2 cup. Add the cream and bring back to a boil for 1 minute. Remove from heat and add the basil, white pepper and butter. Stir until butter is completely emulsified and sauce is shiny.

5 Arrange the fish on four plates and spoon some sauce around each fillet. Serve immediately.

Wine Suggestion - Serve with Silver Canyon Chardonnay.

TALLEY VINEYARDS

Talley Vineyards is a family owned vineyard and winery that specializes in estate-grown Chardonnay and Pinot Noir of uncompromised quality. Located in the Arroyo Grande Valley on California's Central Coast eight miles inland from the Pacific Ocean, the vineyard lies south of the Edna Valley and north of Santa Barbara county. The marine influence makes the Arroyo Grande Valley one of the coolest and most temperate viticultural areas in California, resulting in a long and mild growing season well suited for premium Chardonnay and Pinot Noir production.

The Talley family has farmed vegetables in the fertile valley since 1948 when Talley Farms was founded by Oliver Talley. Today second-and-third generation family members control operations at the farm and vineyard. The first vines for the vineyard were planted in 1982, and to date, there are 102 acres of vineyards. In 1986, 450 cases were produced. Current production is 5,000 cases annually.

At Talley Vineyards the emphasis is on maintaining consistency of style from vintage to vintage that can only be achieved with estate-grown grapes and total control over winemaking operations.

✂ *For an elegant presentation, have the butcher French the bones (scrape away the thin strip of meat and fat from the ends to the eye), leaving the bare bones, which can be dressed at serving time with little paper booties. Serve with roasted new potatoes and fresh asparagus.*

ROASTED RACK OF LAMB WITH PINOT NOIR SAUCE
6 portions

Marinade
1 1/2 cups Talley Vineyards Sauvignon Blanc
1/4 cup extra virgin olive oil
1 cup coarsely chopped onion
1 tablespoon minced fresh thyme
1 tablespoon minced fresh marjoram
10 cracked black peppercorns
1 bay leaf

Lamb
2 racks of lamb, 9 ribs per rack
Salt and freshly ground black pepper, to taste

Pinot Noir Sauce
1 3/4 cup beef stock, preferably homemade, or 1 can
    (14 1/2 ounce) beef broth
1 cup Talley Vineyards Pinot Noir
3 tablespoons unsalted butter
2 shallots, peeled and finely minced
1 tablespoon flour
Reserved pan juices from the lamb

For the marinade

1   Combine all the ingredients for the marinade in a large bowl and stir well.

2   Trim all visible fat from the lamb racks and discard the fat. Add the lamb racks to the marinade. Cover and let marinate at room temperature for 3 to 4 hours.

3   Remove the lamb from the marinade and pat dry with paper towels. Set the lamb on a rack in a roasting pan and season it well with the salt and freshly ground black pepper.

4   Preheat the oven to 450°F.

For the lamb

1   Roast the lamb racks for 20 to 25 minutes or until an instant reading thermometer inserted into the thickest part of the meat registers 130°F. for medium-rare. Let the lamb rest while the Pinot Noir sauce is being prepared.

For the sauce

1   Combine the beef stock and the Talley Vineyards Pinot Noir in a saucepan. Cook rapidly over high heat until the volume is reduced by 1/2.

2   In another saucepan melt the butter. Add the shallots and sauté over low heat for 10 minutes, until the shallots are limp. Add the flour and cook, stirring for 3 minutes. Add the reduced beef stock and whisk over medium heat until the sauce is slightly thickened. Add the pan juices from the lamb racks.

3   Pour the sauce through a fine mesh sieve, pressing hard on the solids to extract all the juices. Keep the sauce warm while preparing the lamb.

4   Transfer the lamb to a cutting board and slice each lamb rack into individual chops. For each portion, spoon a little of the sauce on a warm dinner plate, and place 3 chops on top of the sauce. Serve immediately.

Wine Suggestion - Serve this elegant entrée with Talley Vineyards Pinot Noir.

VENTANA VINEYARDS

Under the ownership and guidance of Doug Meador, the Ventana Vineyards were planted in the early 1970's beside the Arroyo Seco River in Central Monterey County. The first small commercial picking of grapes in 1977 garnered immediate gold medal recognition for both Chardonnay and Riesling. This record has been maintained as the vineyards have matured and developed.

It is the gentle combination of innovation, research and artistic vision that has set Ventana Vineyards apart from all others. As new techniques are incorporated within the natural attributes of the Monterey County growing conditions, Ventana Vineyards continues to set new standards of excellence. This eternal quest remains the driving force behind the viticulture philosophy of Meador and Ventana. Together they have brought new levels of wine quality to the American table at an affordable price.

✗The unusual ingredients in this recipe are the key to its success. The slight intensity of the garlic, coupled with the salty edge of the cheese heighten the spicy qualities of the wine, making it all come together in the sauce. A generous dish to share in the party spirit. This recipe is from Chef Michael Kimmel of Tarpy's Roadhouse Restaurant next to Ventana Vineyards Tasting Room in Monterey.

ROASTED MONTEREY BAY SALMON IN RIESLING SAUCE
6 portions

Salmon
6 salmon fillets (7 ounces each), skinned, and
    pin-boned
8 tablespoons (1 stick) unsalted butter
Freshly squeezed juice of 1 lemon
2 teaspoons Kosher salt
1 teaspoon freshly ground black pepper
1/4 cup Ventana Vineyards Dry Johannisberg Riesling

Johannisberg Riesling Sauce
2 cups Ventana Vineyards Dry Johannisberg Riesling
1 shallot, peeled and finely chopped
2 cloves garlic, finely minced
2 sprigs fresh thyme
3 sprigs Italian parsley
1 cup heavy or whipping cream
1 pound (4 sticks) unsalted butter, room temperature
2 lemons, freshly grated zest and juice
Kosher salt, to taste
Freshly ground white pepper, to taste
1/4 cup freshly grated Parmesan or Asiago cheese
2 Roma tomatoes, seeded and diced, for garnish

To make the salmon

1   Preheat the oven to 400ºF. Place the salmon on a non-stick baking pan. Set aside.

2   In a 2 cup microwave-proof measuring bowl add the butter, lemon juice, salt, pepper and wine. Cook on high power for 3 to 5 minutes, or until the butter is melted. Stir well and brush on the salmon.

3   Bake the salmon for 5 to 7 minutes, or until the fish is of the desired doneness. Keep warm.

To make the sauce

1   Combine the Dry Johannisberg Riesling, shallot, garlic, thyme and parsley in a saucepan. Cook rapidly over high heat until the liquid has almost all evaporated, 5 to 7 minutes. Watch carefully.

2   Add the cream and cook over medium-high heat until the mixture has reduced and thickened slightly, about 5 minutes. Remove the pan from the heat and strain the sauce in to a smaller saucepan. Set it aside until you are ready to serve the sauce.

3   Just before serving place the sauce over medium heat and add the butter in 2 batches. Whisk until the butter has melted. Do not boil. Season with the lemon zest, juice, salt, pepper and cheese. Taste and correct seasonings.

4   Place the roasted salmon in the center of a warm plate with your favorite vegetable and rice. Spoon the Riesling Sauce over the fish. Sprinkle with the diced Roma tomatoes for color.

Wine Suggestion - This Monterey Bay Salmon is delicious with Ventana Vineyards Sauvignon Blanc or Dry Johannisberg Riesling.

WHITCRAFT WINERY

Behind Whitcraft Winery is its promise to make the best wine possible without compromise. The wine is hand-made using "old-world" methods, with little or no chemicals and minimal processing. The Pinots are never pumped, fined or filtered, and they foresee a time where this will be true for the Chardonnay as well. Careful racking by gas or gravity is carried out for the entire life of the Pinot and for most of the Chardonnay's life, which they believe to be the best technique.

The Whitcraft label is the result of a lead-etched image, hand-printed on a Heidelberg press. The corks are the best in the world (and are very expensive) and will reduce problems of corked bottles by 95 percent. The wines are made with great care in small amounts, as if Chris Whitcraft were to drink each bottle himself. Future plans include growth to 2,000 to 2,500 cases maximum. The winery would rather grow gradually, well below demand, and never compromise its ideals. Whitcraft Winery makes its wines by end results, not the bottom line.

A butterflied leg of lamb cooks in a third the usual time and is a breeze to carve. It is also easier to reach that perfect degree of pinkness with a butterfly cut. Because this lamb is cooked in the oven, it can be enjoyed year round, rain or shine. Serve with steamed green beans and tomatoes Provençale, baked with fresh bread crumbs and herbs.

WHITCRAFT BUTTERFLIED LEG OF LAMB
8 portions

2 large cloves garlic, finely minced
1/2 teaspoon salt
2 tablespoons Dijon mustard
1 tablespoon soy sauce or tamari
1 1/2 teaspoons ground rosemary, thyme or oregano
2 tablespoons freshly squeezed lemon juice
1/4 cup olive oil or peanut oil
1 butterflied leg of lamb (4 to 5 pounds)

1 Combine the garlic, salt, Dijon mustard, soy sauce, rosemary and lemon juice in a blender. With the motor running, add the olive oil through the top in a slow, steady stream until a mayonnaise-like cream consistency is reached.

2 Run two long metal skewers through the lamb to keep it in place. Using a basting brush, paint both sides of the lamb with the mustard-soy-lemon coating, reserving 2 tablespoons for the final cooking. Refrigerate the meat for at least 1 hour or overnight.

3   Preheat the broiler. Brown the lamb, about 4-inches from the heat source, for 10 minutes on each side, basting several times with the mustard-soy-lemon mixture.

4   Remove the lamb from the broiler, and then preheat the oven to 375°F. Set the lamb skin side up and paint it with the remaining mustard-soy-lemon coating. Roast the lamb for 15 to 20 minutes in the upper third of the preheated oven.

5   Remove the meat from the oven and let it sit 10 to 15 minutes before carving so the juices can be reabsorbed back into the tissues.

6   Carve in slanting slices across the grain and moisten with accumulated pan juices.

Wine Suggestion - Serve with Whitcraft Pinot Noir.

YORK MOUNTAIN WINERY

Established in 1882, on land originally deeded by president Ulysses S. Grant, York Mountain Winery produces wines that have, for more than a century, made its name synonymous with excellence. The tasting room is housed in the original winery building made of hand-formed bricks kiln-baked on the premises. Its timbers were brought to York Mountain from Cayucus, taken from the dismantled pier where the great Northwestern lumber schooners delivered their wares.

When Max Goldman purchased the winery from the York family in 1970, he brought with him more than 51 years of winemaking experience. Max's daughter, Suzanne, runs the tasting room in addition to keeping the winery's records and performing the public relations. His son, Steve, is the winemaker. York Mountain Winery today, as in its past, remains a family operated business dedicated to the small (5,000 cases annually) production of outstanding varietal and generic wines.

✗ *Beef Roulades are a familiar comfort food dressed up for a special meal. This is a classic dinner party dish with lots of flavor. Serve with buttered egg noodles.*

SUZANNE'S ROULADES OF BEEF
6 portions

6 thin strips of pounded flank or round steak, 6x6 inches
1 1/2 cups York Mountain Pinot Noir
3 tablespoons extra virgin olive oil
4 cloves finely minced garlic
1 cup chopped onion
1 red bell pepper, cored and cut into long, thin slices
1 fennel bulb, trimmed and cut into 1/4-inch julienne strips
2 carrots, cut into 1/4-inch julienne strips
1/2 pound wild mushrooms (shiitake, porcini,
    chanterelle, oyster) or button mushrooms, sliced
12 large, fresh basil leaves, finely sliced
Salt and freshly ground black pepper, to taste
Unbleached all-purpose flour for dusting
1 freshly sliced ripe tomato for garnish
6 fresh basil sprigs for garnish

I   Marinate the beef in the Pinot Noir for 4 hours at room temperature or overnight in the refrigerator.

2   In a large, heavy skillet or sauté pan over medium-high heat add one tablespoon of the olive oil. When it is hot add the garlic, onion, red bell pepper, fennel and carrots. Sauté the vegetables for 6 minutes, add the mushrooms and continue cooking until the mushrooms are limp. Remove from the heat, stir in the basil and season with salt and pepper. Transfer the vegetables to a bowl and set aside to cool.

3   Remove the beef from the wine, and pat dry with paper towels. Save the wine for later. Lay the beef roulades flat on a work surface and season lightly with salt and pepper. Spoon some of the vegetable filling onto the center of each one. Fold them up like envelopes, secure with string and set aside. Save any extra vegetable filling.

4   Add the remaining olive oil in a deep skillet over medium heat. Flour the roulades lightly, and brown on all sides. Pour the reserved wine into the skillet, and bring to a boil. Surround with any reserved vegetables.

5   Preheat the oven to 300°F. Place the skillet in the oven and bake the roulades, covered, for 1 hour and 15 minutes. Let the roulades rest for 20 minutes before serving.

6   Place the roulades on a serving platter, and pour the juices over the top. Surround with freshly sliced tomatoes and fresh basil leaves and serve.

Wine Suggestion - Serve with York Mountain Winery Pinot Noir.

Zaca Mesa Winery

The Zaca mesa where Zaca Mesa Winery's vineyards are rooted, is an elevated plateau of serene majesty. It lies within the unique Santa Barbara coastal mountain corridors, softly painted by sunlight and directly cooled by the Pacific wind streams.

For more than a thousand years, its boundaries and beauty were revered by Chumash Indians, and later by Spanish settlers, who called it "La Zaca Mesa." This means the restful place. They have come to believe it is where the gods of the sun, the wind, the earth and the rain convene in harmony, at their own table of peace.

This recipe makes enough to feed a small army. However, it freezes wonderfully. Allow one cup of Red Sauce per person when freezing in smaller amounts. Serve with bread and you have an instant party. Rick Manson of Chef Ricks in Santa Maria prepares this award winning Cioppino to pair with Pinot Noir.

Chef Rick's Prize Winning Cioppino
8 quarts

Seafood Stock
1 onion, chopped
5 bay leaves
1 teaspoon black peppercorns
6 carrots, peeled and chopped
3 cups shrimp or lobster shells, or a combination of both
3 sprigs fresh thyme
3 sprigs fresh basil
5 sprigs fresh dill
1/2 teaspoon each: salt, freshly ground black pepper, garlic powder, onion powder, celery salt, paprika, fennel seeds and cayenne pepper
3 quarts water

Red Sauce
1 pound Italian sausage, casings removed
4 onions, chopped
8 large cloves garlic, finely minced
2 fennel bulbs, finely chopped
6 carrots, peeled and cut into 1/2-inch dice
1 bunch celery, cut into 1/2-inch dice
1 bunch Italian parsley, finely chopped
1 pound mushrooms, sliced

1/2 teaspoon each: salt, freshly ground black pepper,
    garlic powder, onion powder and crushed red pepper
2 cups Atlantic brand clam juice
2 cans (28 ounces) crushed tomatoes
1 can (16 ounces) tomato puree
2 cans (28 ounces) Roma tomatoes
6 bay leaves
1 large sprig fresh basil
3 sprigs each: fresh rosemary, thyme and oregano
2 teaspoons each: fennel seed and paprika
1/2 teaspoon saffron threads
2 cups Zaca Mesa Pinot Noir
1 tablespoon sugar
2 fennel bulbs, trimmed and sliced

Seafood
1/2 pound per person of any combination: Red snapper,
    halibut, large prawns, sea scallops, mussels, clams,
    squid and lobsters

To make seafood stock

1 Place all the stock ingredients in a large stock pot. Bring the stock to a boil. Reduce the heat to low and simmer, covered, for 1 hour. Remove the stock from the heat and strain it through a fine sieve. Reserve for later.

To make the red sauce

1 Brown the sausage in a large stock pot over medium heat. Add the onions, garlic, fennel, carrots, celery, parsley, mushrooms and seasonings. Sauté until the vegetables are tender, about 20 minutes, stirring often.

2 Add the remaining ingredients, except the fennel, and bring to a boil. Reduce the heat to low and simmer, covered, for 1 hour. Remove from the heat and cool.

3 In a food processor fitted with a steel blade or a blender, puree the Red Sauce in small batches. Return the sauce to the stock pot and add the Seafood Stock and sliced fennel. Simmer the Cioppino for about 30 minutes, uncovered, until the flavors blend.

4 At this point, the Cioppino may be refrigerated or frozen. Prior to serving, bring the Cioppino to a boil over medium-high heat. Add your choice of fresh seafood and cook until the seafood is just cooked through. Serve immediately.

Wine Suggestion - Serve with Zaca Mesa Pinot Noir.

CHEF'S CHOICE

✗*In the early 1980's, Mary and I spent three months eating our way through Europe. It was in Belgium that we learned about steak au poivre vert. Despite the fact that we both constantly work on a healthier diet, neither of us can resist this calorie-ridden splurge.*

Beef seems to have fallen out of favor these days with many a gourmet because of the three-letter "F" word. All concerns aside, an occasional steak is still a symbol of indulgence to be savored and enjoyed. The European way of serving meat with a flavored cream sauce is furthered in excess by accompanying it with pommes frites (French fries). Follow this with a nice green salad for good measure.

This recipe can be varied indefinitely by adding different combinations of herbs to the sauce or any other ingredients that would be seasonally available. The cognac softens the aggressiveness of the pepper. Add ginger for technicolor dreams later!

STEAK AU POIVRE VERT
6 portions

6 fillet mignon steaks, about 1/2 pound each
4 tablespoons green peppercorns in brine, well-drained
4 tablespoons unsalted butter
1/2 cup cognac or brandy
1 cup homemade beef or veal stock
1 cup heavy or whipping cream
1 tablespoon freshly squeezed lemon juice
Salt and freshly ground black pepper, to taste

1   Using the side of a heavy cleaver, pound the meat to flatten slightly.

2   Use 2 tablespoons of the green peppercorns and press into each side of the steaks.

3   Melt the butter in a large heavy skillet and sauté the steaks over medium-high heat until brown on the outside but red and juicy on the inside, 3 to 4 minutes per side.

4   Pour off the fat from the skillet and add the cognac or brandy. Flambé the steaks until the flames are extinguished. Transfer the steaks to a large platter and keep warm.

5   Add the stock, cream and the remaining green peppercorns to the skillet. Cook over high heat until thickened enough to coat the back of a spoon, 7 to 9 minutes. Season the sauce with lemon juice, salt and pepper. Spoon the sauce over the steaks and serve immediately.

Wine Suggestion - Enjoy this dish with a red wine that has black pepper nuances, perhaps a full-bodied Pinot Noir, Zinfandel or Syrah.

$\mathcal{D}$ESSERTS

ARCIERO WINERY

Frank and Phil Arciero immigrated from Italy more than 50 years ago. Their dream of opening a winery was realized in 1986. The Arciero families are actively involved in the vineyard and the operation of the winery, with a strong and steady commitment. With a production of 75,000 cases, the Arciero Winery is one of the largest estate wineries in Paso Robles, producing varietals conducive to the ideal climatic conditions of this region.

The Arciero Winery and Tasting Room of Italian-Mediterranean design is one of California's most spectacular new wineries. Located midway between San Francisco and Los Angeles, the 78,000 square foot facility houses state-of-the-art winemaking equipment, a sophisticated laboratory, and case goods warehouse. Tours are available for guests on the self-guided tour walk. Visitors may also sample wine in the tasting room adjacent to the winery and picnic area on the beautiful grounds overlooking the estate vineyard and rose garden.

✗ *This recipe combines fruits with a traditional cheesecake, which paired with the Late Harvest Muscat Canelli makes a satisfying finale to any meal.*

❦

ARCIERO FRUIT CHEESECAKE
6 portions

Crust
8 whole graham crackers
2 tablespoons packed brown sugar
4 tablespoons unsalted butter, at room temperature

Filling
8 ounces cream cheese
1/2 cup sugar
1/2 teaspoon vanilla extract
1 tablespoon freshly squeezed lemon juice
2 eggs

Topping
1/2 cup sour cream
1 tablespoon sugar
*1 basket fresh strawberries, rinsed, hulled, and sliced
    vertically*
2 kiwis, peeled, and sliced
3 tablespoons strained apricot jam, warmed
1 tablespoon Arciero Late Harvest Muscat Canelli

1 Preheat the oven to 350°F.

2 Butter a 9-inch pie pan.

3 In a food processor fitted with a steel blade combine the graham crackers, brown sugar, and butter and process thoroughly.

4 Press the mixture into the 9-inch pie pan, covering the bottom and reaching almost up the sides.

Prepare the filling

1 Combine the cream cheese, sugar, vanilla and lemon juice in the bowl of a food processor fitted with a steel blade and cream thoroughly. Add the eggs and process until well blended.

2 Pour the mixture into the prepared crust and bake until almost set, about 40 minutes. Remove it from the oven and allow it to cool for several minutes.

Prepare the topping

1 Stir the sour cream and sugar together in a bowl, then spoon the mixture over the cheesecake.

2 Return the cheesecake to the oven and bake another 10 minutes. Let the cheesecake cool completely, and then finish the fruit topping.

3 Arrange the sliced strawberries and kiwis in a decorative pattern on top of the cheesecake. Stir the apricot jam together with the Muscat Canelli. Using a pastry brush, paint the surface of the fruit with the jam, until all the surface is glazed. Refrigerate for at least 2 hours before serving.

Wine Suggestion - Serve with Arciero Late Harvest Muscat Canelli.

Concannon Vineyard

During the 19th century pioneer vintners discovered the Livermore Valley. Soon they found the valley's climate and soils were very similar to those of the Grave winemaking region of Bordeaux, France.

It was here in 1883 that Irish immigrant James Concannon planted the first vines of Concannon's estate vineyard on the best of Livermore's gravelly soil. Today the estate vineyard remains as it was in 1883 and surrounds the winery and the Concannon family home.

✗ This recipe is from Scottie McKinney, the chef at Wente Brothers. The ganache is so rich that a small amount is plenty. The Raspberry Sauce is the perfect balance of acid to off set the white chocolate.

Concannon White Chocolate Ganache With Raspberry Sauce
12 portions

Ganache
1 pound white chocolate
1/2 cup unsalted butter
1/4 cup Riesling, at room temperature
Raspberry Sauce (recipe follows)

Raspberry Sauce
2 cups fresh or frozen raspberries
2 to 3 tablespoons sugar
1 tablespoon Riesling
1 tablespoon Chambord or raspberry liqueur

For the ganache

1 Melt the white chocolate in the top of a double boiler, over simmering water.

2 Add the butter, stirring constantly, until all of the butter is incorporated into the white chocolate.

3 Add the wine slowly, continuing to stir steadily, until all of the wine is incorporated. If the mixture separates, remove the top of the double boiler from the heat and stir with a wire whip until the Ganache comes back together.

4 Pour the Ganache into 12 lightly oiled small ramekins, or candy molds. Chill for several hours or overnight. Take the Ganache out of the refrigerator 1 hour before serving to soften. Serve with Raspberry Sauce.

For the raspberry sauce

1   Combine all the ingredients in a food processor fitted with a steel blade, or in a blender, and mix until smooth. Refrigerate until ready to serve.

2   To serve, spoon a few tablespoons of the raspberry sauce on a plate and unmold 1 ramekin on top of the sauce.

Wine Suggestion - Serve with Concannon Johannisberg Riesling, Late Harvest Riesling or a Sparkling Wine.

HARMONY CELLARS

Harmony Cellars is a small family owned winery committed to producing fine wines of the highest quality. The tasting room is located in the quaint artisan town of Harmony, population 18, just ten miles south of the Hearst Castle. A new winery facility, overlooking the beautiful Harmony Valley, was completed in June of 1993.

Harmony Cellars first opened its doors in June of 1989 producing Chardonnay, Cabernet Sauvignon, Pinot Noir, Johannisberg Riesling and White Zinfandel varietals. Our Zinjolais (Beaujolais-style Zinfandel) and Noel Vineyards (Christmas Blush) are wines unique to Harmony Cellars. Present production is 3,500 cases with a future production limited to 7,000 cases.

✗ *These crepes are quite simple to prepare, yet they look and taste marvelous.*

❧

JOHANNISBERG RIESLING RAISIN CREPES
6 portions

Dessert Crepes
1 1/4 cups flour
2 tablespoons sugar
3 eggs
1 1/2 cups milk
2 tablespoons unsalted butter, melted

Johannisberg Riesling Raisin Filling
1/2 cup plus 1 tablespoon Harmony Cellars
  Johannisberg Riesling
2/3 cup raisins
1 teaspoon grated orange zest
1 teaspoon corn starch
2 tablespoons finely slivered orange zest
2 tablespoons sugar
1 pint French vanilla ice cream

To make the crepes

1 Combine the flour and sugar in the bowl of a food processor fitted with a steel blade and process briefly.

2 With the motor running, add the eggs, milk and butter through the feed tube. Process until smooth.

3 Let the batter stand at room temperature or in the refrigerator for 1 hour.

4 Heat a heavy 8-inch non-stick skillet over medium heat until quite hot. Pour in 3 tablespoons of the batter, then quickly tilt the pan so the batter spreads evenly, forming a crepe. Cook until lightly brown, about 30 to 45 seconds; then turn and cook another 15 seconds.

5 Repeat, using up all the batter. As you finish the crepes stack them on top of one another. When they cool, wrap the stacked crepes in plastic wrap. They will stay fresh in the refrigerator for 2 days or can be frozen for up to 1 month. Makes 12 crepes.

To make the sauce

1 Pour the 1/2 cup Johannisberg Riesling over the raisins in a glass or microwavable bowl. Stir in 1 teaspoon grated orange zest and let stand for 1 hour.

2 Mix 1 tablespoon Johannisberg Riesling with the cornstarch, stirring to remove any lumps. Add this to the raisin mixture. Mix thoroughly.

3 Heat the raisin sauce in the microwave on full power until the sauce is just beginning to boil. Stir well and continue cooking until the sauce is thickened and clear. Set aside.

4 Toss the slivered orange rind in a bowl with the sugar until the rind is sugar coated. Set aside.

To assemble

1 Fold each crepe into quarters. Place 2 crepes on each plate so that their points touch in the center of the plate. Place a scoop of French vanilla ice cream in the center of each crepe. Spoon raisin sauce over all and sprinkle with the sugar coated orange zest. Serve immediately.

Variation 1: Substitute 1 teaspoon grated fresh ginger for all the orange zest and add it with the raisins. Finish the crepes with a sprinkle of cinnamon.

Variation 2: Substitute dried cherries for the raisins and add 1 tablespoon Kirsch Liqueur to the soaking wine.

Wine Suggestion - Serve with Harmony Cellars Johannisberg Riesling.

STONY RIDGE WINERY

Stony Ridge Winery is located in the historic Livermore Valley of California. Originally founded in 1975 in the neighboring town of Pleasanton, Stony Ridge relocated to its current home in 1992. The current owners and operators, the Scotto family, have made Stony Ridge a family destination. In conjunction with the winery, the new complex includes a large deck overlooking Livermore vineyards and a small gourmet restaurant that serves lunch Monday through Saturday.

A small, experimental vineyard has been planted in front of the tasting room. Selected clones of the Italian variety Sangiovese from the famed Chianti region in Tuscany will produce the first vintage.

This rich and luxurious cake is almost sinful. It definitely deserves to be called a gateau. *Make this distinguished dessert for a special occasion. This recipe was designed by students at the California Culinary Academy for a Stony Ridge Winery dinner.*

CHOCOLATE GATEAU WITH KIRSCH GANACHE

One cake, 12 to 16 portions

Gateau
9 1/2 ounces bittersweet chocolate
2 tablespoons water
4 tablespoons unsalted butter
4 large eggs, separated, at room temperature
1/2 cup sugar
1 teaspoon vanilla extract
*2 tablespoons sifted potato starch**
Pinch of salt
*1/3 cup ground hazelnuts***

Kirsch Ganache
1 egg yolk
2 tablespoons granulated sugar
1/2 teaspoon vanilla extract
7 ounces bittersweet chocolate
1/2 cup heavy or whipping cream
2 tablespoons Kirsch Liqueur
Unsweetened cocoa for garnish

* *If potato starch is unavailable, substitute 2 tablespoons sifted corn starch.*

** *Roast hazelnuts on a baking sheet in a 350°F. oven for 10 to 15 minutes, or until their skins have loosened. Remove from the oven and rub between towels to remove skins. Transfer to the bowl of a food processor fitted with a steel blade, and run the machine until the nuts are finely chopped, but have not formed a paste.*

Gateau

1 Preheat the oven to 325°F. Butter and flour a 9-inch spring form pan and tap out any excess flour.

2 Grate or break chocolate into small pieces. Place in top part of a double boiler with the water. Melt over simmering water, whisking until smooth. Add the butter 1 tablespoon at a time until it is incorporated. Let chocolate cool slightly.

3 Beat the egg yolks with half of the granulated sugar until they are thick and pale yellow and form a ribbon when they fall from the beater. Fold in the vanilla, potato starch, salt, ground hazelnuts and chocolate mixture. Mix thoroughly but gently.

4 Beat egg whites until soft peaks form, add the remainder of the sugar and continue beating until stiff peaks form. Add this mixture to the chocolate mixture; fold together gently, incorporating whites completely. Be very careful at this stage not to overmix.

5 Turn batter into the spring form pan. Set on the middle rack of the oven and bake for 50 minutes, or until a toothpick inserted in center comes out clean. Cool on a rack for 15 minutes, then remove outer rim. Allow cake to cool completely, and then refrigerate.

Ganache

1 In a mixing bowl, whip the egg yolk, sugar, and vanilla until light and fluffy. Set aside.

2 Grate or break the chocolate into small pieces. Add the cream to the chocolate and cook over very low heat until the chocolate is just melted or a candy thermometer registers 115°F.

3 Stir the cream and chocolate into the egg yolk mixture, then add the Kirsch Liqueur and blend well.

To glaze the cake

1 Set the cake on a wire rack over a baking sheet (to catch the drips). Spoon the glaze over the cake and spread it over the top and sides. Transfer the cake to a serving platter and refrigerate until the glaze is set, about 2 hours.

2 To serve, sift a little of the unsweetened cocoa over the top of the cake for garnish and flavor. This cuts the sweetness of the cake, enhancing the pairing with the Merlot.

Wine Suggestion - Serve with Stony Ridge Winery North Coast Merlot.

CHEF'S CHOICE

✄ *This recipe came to us from Toni Impala, a dear friend and premier caterer. Toni, who is southern Italian, was given this recipe from a friend in Tuscany. It is the essence of simplicity and a nice way to end a heavy or rich meal. The flavor improves with overnight refrigeration, and you can serve it with whipped cream, ice cream, cookies, biscotti or by itself.*

Keep in mind that fruits are seasonal and choose fruits that complement each other in color, flavor and texture. The fruits listed below are suggestions, add or subtract any combination that appeals to you. Remember, good quality and freshness are the key to this dessert.

❦

FRESH FRUIT IN A WINE SAUCE
12 portions

Wine Sauce
1 cup sugar
2 cups water
1 lemon, zest and juice
Grated zest of 1 orange
1 cup semi-dry white wine such as Chenin Blanc,
*   Riesling or Sparkling Wine*

Summer Fruit Combination
1 pineapple, peeled, cored and cut into 1/2-inch dice
1 cantaloupe, peeled, seeded and cut into 1/2-inch dice
1 honeydew, peeled, seeded and cut into 1/2-inch dice
3 freestone peaches, pitted and cut into 1/2-inch dice
4 ripe plums, pitted and cut into 1/2-inch dice
2 baskets strawberries,* hulled and quartered
2 kiwi fruits,* peeled and sliced

Winter Fruit Combination
1 pineapple, peeled, cored and cut into 1/2-inch dice
6 Delicious apples, cored and cut into 1/2-inch dice
6 navel oranges, peeled, sectioned and cut into 1/2-
*   inch dice*
4 ripe pears, cored and cut into 1/2-inch dice
1 basket raspberries*, lightly rinsed, drained and
*   picked over*
3 kiwi fruits*, peeled and sliced

Fresh mint leaves and edible flowers to garnish

* These fruits should be added just before serving to preserve the color and flavors of the finished dish.

1 In a medium saucepan combine the sugar and the water. Bring to boil over medium heat. Add the lemon zest and juice and the orange zest. Reduce the heat to low and simmer the syrup for 20 minutes.

2 Add the wine to the syrup and return to a boil. Simmer for an additional five minutes. Strain the syrup through a fine mesh sieve into a large mixing bowl.

3 Add the fruit to the syrup beginning with the pineapple and the citrus fruits. Add the other fruits as you are cutting them. Using a rubber spatula, gently stir the fruits coating them well with the syrup. Place the fruits in a non-reactive bowl or plastic container and refrigerate overnight.

4 Just before serving add the remaining fruits to the mixture and gently fold them together. To serve place the fruits in a cut-glass bowl or in individual stemmed glasses. Spoon some of the juices over the top and garnish as desired. Serve immediately.

Wine Suggestion - Any white dessert wine with some residual sugar complements this dessert.

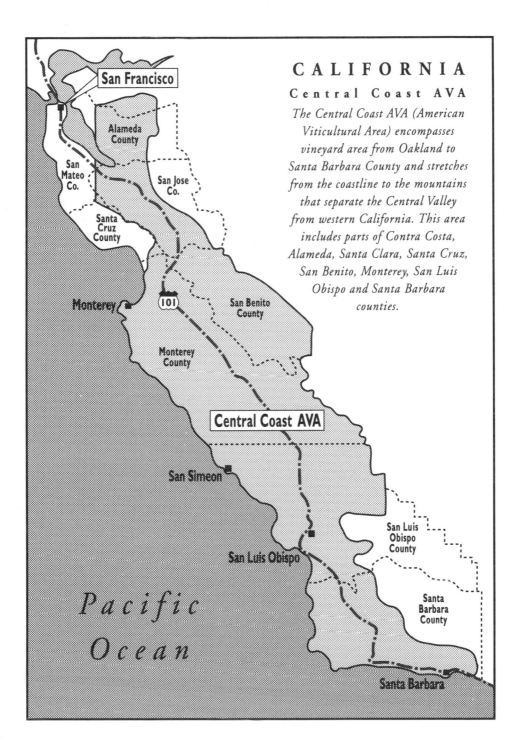

CALIFORNIA
Central Coast AVA

The Central Coast AVA (American Viticultural Area) encompasses vineyard area from Oakland to Santa Barbara County and stretches from the coastline to the mountains that separate the Central Valley from western California. This area includes parts of Contra Costa, Alameda, Santa Clara, Santa Cruz, San Benito, Monterey, San Luis Obispo and Santa Barbara counties.

San Francisco

Alameda County

San Mateo Co.

San Jose Co.

Santa Cruz County

Monterey

101

San Benito County

Monterey County

Central Coast AVA

San Simeon

San Luis Obispo County

San Luis Obispo

Santa Barbara County

Pacific Ocean

Santa Barbara

WINERY NAME	STREET ADDRESS	CITY STATE ZIP PH./FX.
Adelaida Cellars	5805 Adelaida Rd. (805) 239-8980 / (800) 676-1232 / fax (805) 239-4671	Paso Robles, CA 93446
Alban Vineyards	8575 Orcutt Rd. (805) 546-0305 / fax (805) 546-9879	Arroyo Grande, CA 93420
Arciero Winery	P.O. Box 1287 (805) 239-2562 / fax (805) 239-2317	Paso Robles, CA 93447
Au Bon Climat Winery	Box 113 (805) 937-9801	Los Olivos, CA 93441
Babcock Vineyards	5175 Hwy. 246 (805) 736-1455 / fax (805) 736-3886	Lompoc, CA 93436
Baileyana Winery	5880 Edna Rd. (805) 544-9080 / fax (805) 546-0413	San Luis Obispo, CA 93401
The Brander Vineyard	2401 Refugio Rd. / P.O. Box 92 (805) 688-2455 / fax (805) 688-8010	Los Olivos, CA 93441
Buttonwood Farm Winery	1500 Alamo Pintado Rd. (805) 688-3032 / fax (805) 688-6168	Solvang, CA 93463
Byron Vineyard & Winery	5230 Tepusquet Rd. (805) 937-7288 / fax (805) 937-1246	Santa Maria, CA 93454
Carey Cellars	1711 Alamo Pintado Rd. (805)688-8554 / fax (805) 688-9327	Solvang, CA 93463
Casa De Fruta	6680 Pacheco Pass Hwy. (408) 637-0051 / fax (408) 637-1293	Hollister, CA 95023
Castoro Cellars	1480 No. Bethel Rd. (805) 238-0725 / fax (805) 434-0580	Templeton, CA 93465
Cedar Mountain Winery	7000 Tesla Rd. (510) 373-6636 / fax (510) 373-6694	Livermore, CA 94550
Chateau Julien Winery	8940 Carmel Valley Rd. (5 miles off Hwy 1) (408) 624-2600 / fax (408) 624-6138	Carmel, CA 93922
Chouinard Vineyards	33853 Palomares (510) 582-9900 / fax (510) 733-6274	Castro Valley, CA 94552
Claiborne & Churchill Vintners	860 Capitolio Way (805) 544-4066	San Luis Obispo, CA 93401
Concannon Vineyard	4590 Tesla Rd. (510) 447-3760 / fax (510) 447-2725	Livermore, CA 94550
Corbett Canyon Vineyards	2195 Corbett Canyon Rd. (805) 544-5800 / fax (805) 544-7205	Arroyo Grande, CA 93420
Cottonwood Canyon Vineyard & Winery	P.O. Box 3459 (805) 549-9463 / fax (805) 546-8031	San Luis Obispo, CA 93403-3459
Creston Vineyards	P.O. Box 577 (805) 434-1399 / fax (805) 434-2426	Templeton, CA 93465

Eberle Winery	Hwy 46 East / P.O. Box 2459 (805) 238-9607 / fax (805) 237-0344	Paso Robles, CA 93447
Edna Valley Vineyard	2585 Biddle Ranch Rd. (805) 544-9594 / fax (805) 544-0112	San Luis Obispo, CA 93401
Emerald Bay Winery	P.O. Box 221775 (408) 624-2600 / fax (408) 624-6138	Carmel, CA 93922
Firestone Vineyard	5017 Zaca Station Rd. (805) 688-3940 / fax (805) 686-1256	Los Olivos, CA 93441
The Gainey Vineyard	3950 E. Hwy 246 / P.O. Box 910 (805) 688-0558 / fax (805) 688-5864	Santa Ynez, CA 93460
Garland Ranch Winery	P.O. Box 221775 (408) 624-2600 / fax (805) 624-6138	Carmel, CA 93922
Georis Winery	P.O. Box 702 (408) 625-6731 / fax (408) 625-0409	Carmel, CA 93921
Harmony Cellars	3255 Harmony Valley Rd. (805) 927-1625	Harmony, CA 93435
Hecker Pass Winery	4605 Hecker Pass Hwy. (408) 842-8755	Gilroy, CA 95020
JanKris Winery	Route 2, Box 40-B, Bethel Rd. (805) 434-0319 / fax (805) 434-0509	Templeton, CA 93465
Justin Vineyards & Winery	11680 Chimney Rock Rd (805) 238-6932 / fax (805) 238-7382	Paso Robles, CA 93446
Lane Tanner Winery	RT 1, Box 144A (805) 934-0230	Santa Maria, CA 93454
Leeward Winery	2784 Johnson Dr. (805) 656-5054 / fax (805) 656-5092	Ventura, CA 93003
Livermore Valley Cellars	1508 Wetmore Rd. (510) 447-1751	Livermore, CA 94550
Maison Deutz Sparkling Winery	453 Deutz Dr. (805) 481-1763 /fax (805) 481-6920	Arroyo Grande, CA 93420
Martin Brothers Winery	P.O. Box 2599 (805) 238-2520 / fax (805) 238-6041	Paso Robles, CA 93447
Meridian Vineyards	7000 Hwy 46 East / P.O. Box 3289 (805) 237-6000 / fax (805) 239-5715	Paso Robles, CA 93447
Mosby Winery	9496 Santa Rosa Rd. / P.O. Box 1849 (805) 688-2415 / fax (805)686-4288	Buelton, CA 93427
The Ojai Vineyard	P.O. Box 952 (805) 687-4967 / fax (805) 687-2342	Oakview, CA 93022
Paraiso Springs Vineyards	38060 Paraiso Springs Rd. (408) 678-0300 / fax (408) 678-2584	Soledad, CA 93960
Paul Masson Vineyards	P.O. Box 780 (408) 675-2481 / fax (408) 675-2611	Gonzales, CA 93926

Peachy Canyon Winery | Peachy Canyon Rd. | Paso Robles, CA   93446
(805) 237-1577 / fax (805) 237-1577

Pesenti Winery | 2900 Vineyard Dr. | Templeton, CA   93465
(805) 434-1030

Piedra Creek Winery | 6238 Orcutt Rd. | San Luis Obispo, CA   93401
(805) 541-1281

Retzlaff Vineyards | 1356 S. Livermore Ave. | Livermore, CA   94550
(510) 447-8941

Sanford Winery | 7250 Santa Rosa Rd. | Buelton, CA   93427
(805) 688-3300 / fax (805) 688-7381

Santa Barbara Winery | 202 Anacapa St. | Santa Barbara, CA   93101
(805) 963-3633 / (800) 225-3633 / fax (805) 962-4981

Saucelito Canyon Vineyards | 1600 Saucelito Creek Rd | Arroyo Grande, CA   93420
Tasting Room 3031 Lopez Dr. | Arroyo Grande, CA   93420
(805) 489-8762

Silver Canyon Estate Wines | 1901 Avenue of the Stars, Ste. #930 | Los Angeles, CA   90067
(310) 282-0733 / fax (310) 201-6581

Stony Ridge Winery | 4948 Tesla Rd. | Livermore, CA   94550
(510) 449-0660 / fax (510) 449-0646

Talley Vineyards | 3031 Lopez Dr. | Arroyo Grande, CA   93420
(805) 489-0446 / fax (805) 489-0996

Thomas Kruse Winery | 4390 Hecker Pass Rd. | Gilroy, CA   95020
(408) 842-7016

Tobin James Cellars | 8950 Union Rd. | Paso Robles, CA   93446
(805) 239-2204

Twin Hills Winery | 2025 Nacimiento Lake Dr. | Paso Robles, CA   93446
(805) 238-9148 / fax (805) 239-3060

Ventana Vineyards | 2999 Monterey-Salinas Hwy. | Monterey, CA   93940
(408) 372-7415 / fax (408) 655-1855

Wente Bros. Winery | 5565 Tesla Rd. | Livermore, CA   94550
(510) 447-3603 / fax (510) 447-2972

Whitcraft Winery | 860 E. Stowell Rd., Ste. W | Santa Maria, CA   93454
(805) 965-3424

Wild Horse Winery & Vineyards | 1437 Wild Horse Winery Court | Templeton, CA   93465
(805) 434-2541 / fax (805) 434-3516

Windemere Wines | 6262 Orcutt Rd. | San Luis Obispo, CA   93401
(805) 473-3836

York Mountain Winery | York Mountain Rd., RT2 Box 191 | Templeton, CA   93465
(805) 238-3925

Zaca Mesa Winery | 6905 Foxen Canyon Rd. / P.O. Box 899 | Los Olivos, CA   93441-0899
(805) 688-3310 / fax (805) 688-8796

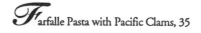

RECIPE INDEX

For more
information
about

call
805•549•8532